Urban Government for Metropolitan Lagos

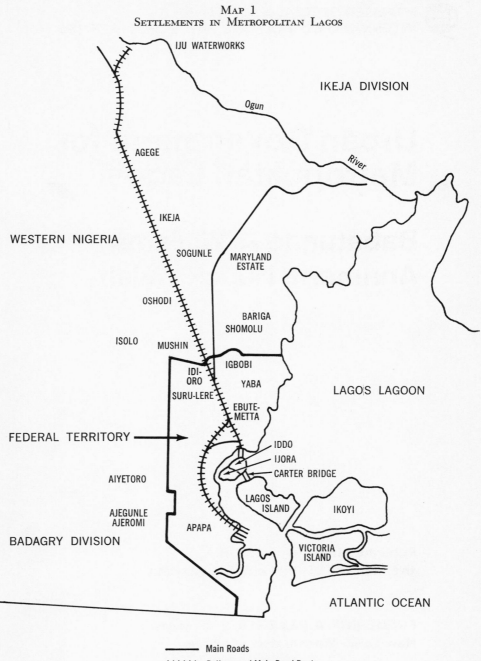

MAP 1
SETTLEMENTS IN METROPOLITAN LAGOS

IJU WATERWORKS

IKEJA DIVISION

Ogun

AGEGE

River

IKEJA

WESTERN NIGERIA

SOGUNLE

MARYLAND
ESTATE

OSHODI

BARIGA
SHOMOLU

ISOLO

MUSHIN

IDI-
ORO

IGBOBI

YABA

LAGOS LAGOON

SURU-LERE

EBUTE-
METTA

FEDERAL TERRITORY →

IDDO
IJORA
CARTER BRIDGE

AIYETORO

LAGOS
ISLAND

IKOYI

AJEGUNLE
AJEROMI

APAPA

BADAGRY DIVISION

VICTORIA
ISLAND

ATLANTIC OCEAN

——— Main Roads
+++++ Railway and Main Road Route

PRAEGER SPECIAL STUDIES IN
INTERNATIONAL POLITICS AND PUBLIC AFFAIRS

Urban Government for Metropolitan Lagos

Babatunde A. Williams
braham
Annmarie Hauck Walsh

Published in cooperation with
the Institute of Public Administration

FREDERICK A. PRAEGER, Publishers
New York · Washington · London

The purpose of the Praeger Special Studies is to make specialized re-search monographs in U.S. and international economics and politics available to the academic, business, and government communities. For further information, write to the Special Projects Division, Frederick A. Praeger, Publishers, 111 Fourth Avenue, New York, N.Y. 10003.

This book is No. 2 in the series *The International Urban Studies of the Institute of Public Administration.*

FREDERICK A. PRAEGER, PUBLISHERS
111 Fourth Avenue, New York, N.Y. 10003, U.S.A.
77-79 Charlotte Street, London W.1, England

Published in the United States of America in 1968
by Frederick A. Praeger, Inc., Publishers

Library of Congress Catalog Card Number: 67-22285

Printed in the United States of America

FOREWORD

Comparative administration, particularly comparative urban administration, is a young field of study. It has arisen in part as a response to the need for comparative data and information on administrative improvement for purposes of technical assistance and in part from the interest of scholars in accumulating knowledge and formulating generalizations having cross-national validity.

This study of the government and administration of metropolitan Lagos is intended to supply detailed information on how a particular area is organized to cope with expanding needs generated by urban growth and economic development and to identify problems relevant to such organization. It is one in a series of twelve case studies of urban areas in as many countries in Africa, Asia, Europe, North America, and South America. The studies have been conducted by the Institute of Public Administration (IPA) with the assistance of a grant for international urban studies from the Ford Foundation, and in collaboration with the United Nations. The aim of the series is to present comparable data and descriptive analyses of the structure of urban government and public administration in areas with widely varying political, economic, and cultural systems. An important objective is to provide students and scholars with materials from which to develop comparative insights and hypotheses on the administrative aspects of urbanization. As another part of the project, IPA has prepared for the Division for Public Administration of the United Nations a comparative analysis of certain aspects of the case studies, concentrating on material of particular interest to less-developed countries.

This study of metropolitan Lagos was made possible by the co-sponsorship and support of the Institute of Administration, University of Ife, Ibadan. It is based on analysis of documentation and interviews undertaken according to a detailed, uniform field-work schedule that was used for each of the case areas. The field work in each area was handled by a resident expert thoroughly familiar with local conditions. In Lagos, it was conducted during 1964-65, but the major events of 1966 have been incorporated into the report.

We are most grateful to those persons in Lagos who consented to be interviewed and who generously provided data, particularly Chief Engineer Ukpoma, Lagos Water Supply; H. A. Subair, K. MacGregor, and A. O. Craig of the Lagos Executive Development Board; S. O. King, Secretary to the Lagos City Transport Service Board; T. O. Disu, S. A. Folami, and Dr. G. A. Williams, officers of the Lagos City Council. Participants in the project at the Institute included Drs. Joseph E. McLean and Randy H. Hamilton, who at various stages served as project directors; Dr. Frank Smallwood; and Rodman T. Davis. The advice of Emil J. Sady of the United Nations and suggestions from members of the Comparative Urban Studies Section of the Comparative Administration Group (American Society for Public Administration) have been valuable throughout. The project secretary, Anthony Asalone, has labored long and well to help move the work to completion.

Annmarie Hauck Walsh, co-author of this case study and project director, has prepared a comparative overview of the field reports (to be published by Frederick A. Praeger, Inc., in 1968).

Lyle C. Fitch, President
Institute of Public Administration
New York

CONTENTS

		Page
FOREWORD		v
LIST OF MAPS, CHARTS, AND TABLES		ix
LIST OF ABBREVIATIONS		x

Chapter

1 DIMENSIONS OF THE REGION ... 1

The People and the Land ... 3
The Economy ... 12
Political Characteristics ... 17
Conclusions ... 28
Notes to Chapter 1 ... 31

2 GOVERNMENTAL INSTITUTIONS FOR LAGOS ... 32

Government in Nigeria ... 33
The Federal Government in Metropolitan
Lagos ... 37
The Regional Government in Lagos ... 40
Local Government in the Urban Area ... 40
Notes to Chapter 2 ... 53

3 INTERGOVERNMENTAL RELATIONSHIPS ... 54

Allocation of Powers ... 55
Controls by Higher Government ... 61
Metropolitan Relationships ... 65
Notes to Chapter 3 ... 76

Chapter		Page
4	PLANNING FOR LAGOS	77
	Economic Planning	77
	Town and Country Planning	82
	Planning Needs	86
	Plan Implementation	89
	Notes to Chapter 4	93
5	SELECTED URBAN SERVICES IN LAGOS	94
	Water Supply	94
	Mass Passenger Transportation	108
	Public Housing Programs	121
	Education	134
	Notes to Chapter 5	157
6	COMPARATIVE TRENDS AND PROBLEMS IN URBAN ADMINISTRATION	158
	SELECTED BIBLIOGRAPHY	177
	ABOUT THE AUTHORS	183

LIST OF MAPS, CHARTS, AND TABLES

MAPS
Page

1 Settlements in Metropolitan Lagos   ii

CHARTS

1 City Government of Lagos   43

2 Lagos Water Supply Agency   96

3 The Educational System: Federal Territory   138

4 The Educational System: Western Region   139

TABLES

1 Land Use in Selected Settlements   6

2 Lagos Metropolitan Area Population   9

3 Demographic Characteristics   10

4 Number of Schools and Pupils in the City of
   Lagos, By Managing Authority   136

5 Expenditure for Elementary Education in the
   City of Lagos   147

6 Enrollment in Schools by Type   150

LIST OF ABBREVIATIONS

LCTS	Lagos City Transport Service
LEDB	Lagos Executive Development Board
MDA	Metropolitan Development Agency
NCNC	National Council of Nigerian Citizens
NNA	Nigerian National Alliance
NNDP	Nigerian National Democratic Party
NPC	Northern People's Congress
UPGA	United Progressive Grand Alliance
UPP	United People's Party
USAID	United States Agency for International Development
WNHC	Western Nigeria Housing Corporation

Urban Government for Metropolitan Lagos

CHAPTER 1 DIMENSIONS OF THE REGION

Greater Lagos is an urban complex of 1 million people that embodies tremendous contrasts. The capital and major port of the largest nation in Africa, it is a powerful magnet for migrants from all four regions of the federation of some 55 million people. Onto a nucleus of traditional African urban settlements are grafted modern industrial, commercial, and administrative establishments, as well as mushrooming settlements of new entries into the labor force, which extend 20 miles from the city center. Elements of widely spaced centuries and cultures coexist and intermingle: suburban subdivisions of modern, single-family homes and closely packed extended-family compounds without water or paved streets; large, air-conditioned department stores and thousands of street hawkers, market stalls, and tradeswomen bearing trays of cloth, oranges, and toothbrushes on their heads; trade unions and professional associations; kinship meetings and tribal associations; elected councilmen and inherited chieftaincies; factories and subsistence agriculture; office skyscrapers, luxury hotels, and open sewers.

The City of Lagos has become the largest city in Nigeria, slightly outstripping Ibadan, the capital of the Western Region, in the past decade. The Yoruba peoples of the Western Region of Nigeria, of which Lagos was a part until 1954, have a long tradition of urbanism. By 1856, there were ten to twenty cities of over 20,000--including Lagos--in this area, and Ibadan exceeded 100,000 before European contact. As kingdom capitals, many of the traditional cities had extended commercial, agricultural, and political hinterlands. With the introduction of European influence, modern education, and modern economic operations, urbanization accelerated. In the Western Region, 46 per cent of the population lived in towns of 5,000 or more by 1952, a degree of town-dwelling that parallels that found in England in the nineteenth century. In the Western Region, by 1963 there were thirteen

1

towns with populations exceeding 100,000 and twenty-nine exceeding 50,000. The remainder of Nigeria is also experi-
encing rapid urban growth but to date remains predominantly
rural.

There have been three types, then, of urban life in Nigerian history: first, traditional Yoruba cities, which grew
large prior to European contact and embodied folk social systems in urban settlement patterns; second, provincial cities
in Nigeria today, where the traditional settlement patterns
and social systems are still strong but are being gradually
modified by the forces of education, economic development,
and modern government; and third, Lagos and a few new industrial centers, the major parts of which are the product of
modern economic, social, and political forces in interaction
with traditional culture. A significant proportion of the working population of the provincial towns is employed in the agricultural sector, commuting outward to work their fields.
This is not the case in Lagos and the newer industrial centers.

Nigeria's two most pressing problems are political instability and urban poverty in the context of extreme deficiencies in physical facilities and public services (housing, sanitation, water, transport, welfare, etc.). The first problem
limits the ability to mitigate the second. Examination of administration for Lagos presents a study in relief of these two
problems.

While the heart of Lagos is several hundred years old,
the metropolitan complex and modern sector are products of
the past sixty years--and particularly of rapid growth since
Nigeria attained independence in 1960. Like many young
metropolises in developing nations, Lagos does not have the
basic framework of urban infrastructure. It has no closed
sewage systems; extremely limited housing plant; rudimentary road network; the bare beginnings of a public school system; and severely restricted capital resources, for which
many productive investment projects compete. Should the
present growth continue without improvement in these areas,
Lagos will be faced with monumental problems of health and
unemployment, and the pace of economic development will be
affected by deficiencies in transportation and trained manpower.

The demands on urban government are therefore of great urgency. In light of the scarcity of financial resources, if a wide range of large urban investments are to be made in a short period of history, they must be planned in rational and complementary patterns to produce substantial improvement in urban life and economy. Such planning would entail comprehensive urban-design policies, investment programming, as well as careful social planning to protect the assets of traditional social structures while creating institutions and manpower resources for the modern sector.

Two major types of administrative problems compound the difficulties of government in meeting this challenge. The first is an organizational problem that is complicated by political conflict. The metropolitan area includes not only the Federal Territory of Lagos, but also a sizable portion of the Western Region (one of the four constituent regions of the Nigerian Federation). While the greatest service deficiencies are in the Western Region portion of the urban complex, there is no governmental jurisdiction with territorial and functional powers to resolve urban-wide issues, and intergovernmental relationships to this end have been limited and unstable. The second major problem is shortage of administrative resources, particularly experienced professional and managerial manpower.

THE PEOPLE AND THE LAND

The Lagos urban area as here defined includes, first, the City and Federal Territory of Lagos, the boundaries of which coincide. Second, the urban area includes some 40 square miles of the Western Region mainland, in which there are about twelve town-settlements and four local-government units called district councils.

The boundaries of this metropolitan complex are discernible on the basis of both population density and economic patterns, although there is no formal administrative jurisdiction corresponding to it. The metropolitan area is contiguous and its entire expanse is traversable in a few hours; persons living in Agege or Ikeja, at the northern extremity, often work in Apapa, at the southern extremity. Population density falls off radically outside the settlements defined as part of metropolitan Lagos. *

A very small proportion (less than 5 per cent) of the urban area is now devoted to agricultural uses. The City of Lagos itself has only about 3 square miles of undeveloped land, the rest being either built up or planned open space. By contrast, however, there is a good deal of undeveloped land in outer mainland portions of the urban area.

The present configuration of land use in the metropolitan area reflects stages in its growth. The city center is the densely populated Lagos Island, which is a natural port on a lagoon protected from the Atlantic Ocean by a sand bar and two marshy islands to the south. The city (Federal Territory) itself consists, in addition, of Victoria Island to the south, Ikoyi Island to the east, Iddo-Ijora Island to the north, and a north-south strip of mainland from Suru-Lere to Apapa (see Map 1). Mainland settlements comprising the rest of the urban area include: Mushin, Shomolu, Bariga, Iwaya, Oshodi, Sogunle, Isolo, Maryland Estate, Ikeja, and Agege continuing north (all part of the Ikeja Division of the Western Region); and a few fingers of development running west from Apapa to Ajegunle, Ajeromi, and Aiyetoro, which are part of the Badagry Division of the Western Region.

Lagos Island was the site of a traditional city-state that was swelled by refugees fleeing from wars in the north and by conquerors from Benin. Vestiges of traditional settlement patterns are found in the northwestern end of Lagos Island, which consists of single-story, extended-family compounds and market stalls. Its density is more than 500 persons per acre (which, extended, would equal 340,000 persons per square mile) and 36 persons per house.

The port developed on the southern shores of Lagos Island; it was a prominent West African port of call for

------

* The area included in metropolitan greater Lagos, as here described and indicated on Map 1, was identified by a United Nations technical assistance team in 1965. Reference in this study to the urban area or metropolitan Lagos indicates this expanse. See Otto Koenigsberger, et al., Metropolitan Lagos (New York: United Nations Commissioner for Technical Assistance, 1964.)

Spanish and Portuguese merchants, particularly in the slave trade of the seventeenth and eighteenth centuries. During the nineteenth century, commercial trade through the port expanded and new migrant groups were added to the town--repatriated slaves coming from Brazil and Sierre Leone who were Christian and Muslim peoples. These groups, consisting of artisans and persons familiar with Western institutions, became the earliest professional cadres in theology, education, medicine, and law. As intermediaries between Nigerian and European elements, they gave impetus to the expansion of trade. After the establishment of British control in the second half of the nineteenth century, when Lagos became the focal point of both European commerce and administrative control of Nigeria, the southern shore of the island grew steadily as the center of commercial and administrative activities. The southern waterfront is today the commercial center of Lagos, and the eastern end of the island contains governmental and administrative establishments. The major port facilities have moved across the lagoon to Apapa, where the greater part of industrial development has been located.

By 1921, Lagos was a city of nearly 100,000 people, and the island of Ikoyi was being developed into low-density residential neighborhoods for civil service and commercial cadres. Ikeja in the 1940's and Victoria in the 1960's were subject to similar development. Between 1930 and 1960, the urban area tripled in population and spread into the Western Region on a linear pattern along the main paved road and the railroad line.

With Nigerian independence, migration into Lagos gained tremendous momentum. In the last intercensus decade (1952-62), the metropolitan area as a whole grew by 200 per cent; the Western Region portion of the urban area, however, grew by well over 600 per cent--about 66 per cent per year between 1952 and 1962. During this period, the Iddo-Ijora area became the location for secondary industrial, commercial, and service expansion. Industrialization of Apapa took place. Industrial parks were developed in Ikeja, at the northern extremity of the urban complex, and its residential population grew rapidly. Maryland Estate and Victoria were developed as high- and middle-income residential areas; Suru-Lere was constructed by public agencies; much of Ajegunle was reclaimed from swamp. Sections such as

TABLE 1

LAND USE IN SELECTED SETTLEMENTS

LAGOS METROPOLITAN AREA
(percentage)

	Residential			Commercial	Services & Industry	Government	Recreation
	High Density	Medium Density	Low Density				
Lagos Island	45			27		27	
Ikoyi			98	2			
Victoria			85			12 (embassies)	3
Iddo-Ijora-Iganmu		3			97 (mainly services)		
Ebute Metta	98						
Apapa	15	25			60 (import and manufacturing)		

	Residential			Commercial	Services & Industry	Government	Recreation
	High Density	Medium Density	Low Density				
Yaba	75			10	10	5 (education)	
Ajegunle-Ajeromi	98						
Mushin	90			-	10	-	
Ikeja	20	40				40	
Shomolu	98						
Maryland Estate		98					
Suru-Lere	98						

Source: Lagos Executive Development Board, 1965.

Mushin and Ajegunle were crowded with low-income migrants, often without families, seeking wage employment, particularly in industry at Apapa, Iddo-Ijora, and Ikeja.

The result of these waves of development in Lagos is separate clusters of land uses, as shown in Table 1.

Thus, the Lagos urban complex had burst the boundaries of the federal territory and grown to 942,000 inhabitants according to the census of 1962 (see Table 2). While in 1952 almost 90 per cent of the population of metropolitan Lagos lived in the federal territory, at present only about 60 per cent do. The increasing importance of the Western Region portion will continue because of the availability of land, which is abundant both to the east and to the west of the main transportation axis.

In 1952, half of the population of Lagos had been born elsewhere. Moreover, of the growth between 1952 and 1962, for every addition to the population by natural increase, there were roughly three additions by migration--a total of 320,000 migrants in the decade. A large number of these newcomers live in settlements such as Mushin (which jumped from 32,000 population in 1952 to 155,000 in 1962) and Ajeromi (which jumped from 3,900 to 18,000) in overcrowded conditions. They inhabit dwellings built of mud, bamboo, and corrugated iron sheets, lacking common amenities and sanitary conveniences.

Most of the migrants are young people, graduates of primary schools or dropouts from secondary school who are seeking wage employment. Most of them are unskilled but literate. The rural and smaller urban places in Nigeria are losing educated population to the larger urban centers and particularly to Lagos. Thus, in 1952, half of the population of the Lagos federal territory was literate, as compared with approximately 12 per cent of the population of Nigeria as a whole. Most graduates of secondary school settle in Lagos or a few other large cities in Nigeria such as Port Harcourt and Ibadan, attracted by opportunities for higher level jobs and wage earning as well as by the excitement of city life and freedom from the home-town social structure. The Lagos population bulges radically in the working age categories of fifteen to forty-nine, and males outnumber the females, in contrast to the nation-wide pattern (see Table 3).

TABLE 2

LAGOS METROPOLITAN AREA POPULATION

	Area (square miles)	Population	Density (per square mile)
Lagos City			
1931		126,000)	
1952		272,000) +115%	
1962	27	665,000) +145%	25,000
Western Region Portion[a]			
1952		36,000	
1962	40	277,000 +670%	6,900
Total, Urban Area			
1952		308,000	
1962	67	942,000 +200%	14,000

[a] The population of the Western Region portion breaks down as follows:

Ikeja Division

Mushin	115,000
Shomolu	21,500
Sogunle	2,300
Oshodi	9,000
Isolo	2,300
Ikeja	8,100
Maryland Estate	400
Bariga	5,000
Agege	32,000

Badagry Division

Ajegunle	16,400
Ajeromi	18,000
Aiyetoro	7,100

Source: Koenigsberger, et al. , Metropolitan Lagos (1964).

TABLE 3

DEMOGRAPHIC CHARACTERISTICS

CITY OF LAGOS

Population by Sex and Age, 1953[a]

	Male	Female
0 - 6	27,000	28,000
7 - 14	22,000	21,000
15 - 49	86,000	69,000
50 -	6,000	6,000

Deaths per 1,000 population (1963)	8
Births per 1,000 population (1963)	47
Infant Deaths per 1,000 live births (1960)	63
Percentage Literate	49.1%[b]

Ethnic Groups (1952)[c] (1,000's)

Yoruba	196
Ibo	32
Edo	6
Hausa	4
Other Nigerians	20
Foreigners	9

[a] 88 females per 100 males in total. Comparable figures from the 1963 census are not available, but the nature of migration would indicate greater dominance of working-age males by that time.

[b] Comparable figure for Nigeria as a whole is 12.1%.

[c] Later figures are not available, but the proportion of non-Yoruba groups has grown considerably and is far greater in the metropolitan area as a whole than in the central city.
Source: Reports, Census of Nigeria.

Because of the patterns of migration, Lagos embraces
a high degree of ethnic and linguistic heterogeneity, in contrast to most other cities in Nigeria. The four regions of
Nigeria and the cities within them are each dominated by particular ethnic or tribal groupings. The Western Region is
predominantly Ibo; the Northern Region is predominantly
Hausa; and within the Midwestern Region are several minority peoples such as Edos, Urhobos, and Tsekiris. Thus,
Ibadan, which is close in size to Lagos, was nearly 95 per
cent Yoruba in 1952, while the population of Lagos was approximately 65 per cent Yoruba, 10 per cent Ibo, and 25 per
cent other groups. As non-Yoruba immigration has increased
since independence (Ibos constitute the largest bloc of migrants), Lagos is more mixed today.

Since the early 1930's, migrant groups in Lagos have
formed "tribal unions," which have been utilized as social
clubs, welfare organizations, and political party subunits.
They have acculturated new migrants and minimized the isolation of the individual, a social condition often noted in rapidly urbanizing areas. Traditional loyalties to family, clan,
and tribe are channeled into these voluntary associations,
which are based on town, village, or clan of origin. More
than fifty tribal unions in Lagos have regular meetings, raise
dues, and help members in distress, often cooperating with
voluntary and governmental welfare agencies. Their membership embraces all educational and economic levels, from
the illiterate unemployed to the wealthy professional; some
have formed subdivisions based on occupational categories.

In addition, the unions maintain ties with the town of
origin--frequently with a counterpart local-improvement society, to which the urban union sends funds for community
improvements and scholarships. Through this relationship
they transmit modernization forces from Lagos to the rest of
the country. Having been used by colonial administrators for
tax collection and representation on advisory councils, the
tribal unions today compete in vying for government investments in their home areas. As the individual unions joined
regional and ethnic federations in the 1950's, they became
the building blocks in the formation of the major political
parties during the decade prior to independence.

By contrast with the rest of the urban area, the oldest
part of central Lagos is populated for the most part by people
born in Lagos. [1] In this segment of the population, the
extended family remains an important social unit. Among the
heads of households in this section interviewed by Marris,
61 per cent attended regular meetings of kin at which dues
were collected and by which the sick and unemployed were
aided. The custom by which well-to-do individuals help their
relatives either by direct support or by aid in finding employment or obtaining education is widespread in Nigeria. A federal survey in 1960 found that 10 per cent of the total monthly
expenditures by middle-income families was spent on gifts
and maintenance of relatives.

All of these mechanisms of family and social cohesion
have contributed to social stability and well-being during the
process of rapid growth in Lagos, at a period when the government would be hard pressed to provide extensive welfare
services. There are signs, however, that these mechanisms
are weakening. Westernized middle-income families find it
increasingly difficult to fulfill their own ambitions while contributing financially to the welfare needs of their relatives
and social groups. Migration to Lagos since 1950 has been
so extensive as to outstrip the organization and expansion of
migrant associations. And finally, the spatial dispersal of
groups is reducing their organizational tendencies. The result, in places like Mushin, is a social environment conducive to anomie and its correlates of juvenile delinquency and
sporadic violence. There is a potential for government in
Lagos to preserve and utilize the traditional social mechanisms for neighborhood improvement and aided welfare activities. To date, however, there has been little direct cooperation between the administration and such groups. In fact,
some government actions have unwittingly hastened their
weakening. Slum clearance in central Lagos, for example,
scattered kin groups.

THE ECONOMY

The traditional economy of the Western Region was
and is highly specialized by comparison to most preindustrial
societies in Africa. It consists of subsistence agriculture;
production of primary products for sale such as excess food,
cocoa, kolanuts, and palm oil; crafts such as weaving,

pottery, and tailoring; and extensive small-scale commerce and trade. Retail trade in Lagos is still based on individual sellers offering goods in daily retail--and periodic whole-sale--markets. Importing, large-lot wholesale transactions, and several department stores in Lagos are still controlled in large part by Europeans. The bulk of both imported and local merchandise, however, passes through the hands of Ni-gerian middlemen and traders to be sold in the streets and markets in small lots. Women predominate as both buyers and sellers in the market place.

Large-scale wage earning is relatively recent in Ni-geria. In this nation of over 50 million people, the govern-ment estimates that there are approximately 800,000 persons employed by establishments with 10 or more employees. Nearly 12 per cent of this total, or 96,000 persons, are em-ployed in the City of Lagos itself. Other large-scale eco-nomic activities are concentrated in Mushin and Ikeja within metropolitan Lagos and in other major cities such as Port Harcourt, Ibadan, Kano, and Sapele.

The dominance of Lagos in administration, export, and manufacturing is considerable. Between 1956 and 1959, the City of Lagos handled 44 per cent of Nigeria's exports and 68 per cent of its imports, both of which are rapidly ex-panding. Lagos is the headquarters for major federal gov-ernment agencies, public corporations, and related institu-tions. In fact, the government employs about 26,000 persons in the city, which amounts to 28 per cent of employment in establishments with 10 or more employees, and 17 per cent of all wage employment in the city.

In addition, Lagos is the country's leading industrial center. The central city contains more than 200 registered factories, for production of soap, beer, building materials, textiles, steel products, aluminum wares, and motor vehicle assembly, among others. These establishments employ roughly 23,000 persons. With slightly over 1 per cent of the national population, the City of Lagos accounts for roughly 30 per cent of factory employment throughout the country. The economic base of the Lagos metropolitan area as a whole is greater than these figures for the central city indicate, for industrial and commercial establishments are growing in Mu-shin, Ilu-Eju, and Ikeja.

Moreover, the central city of Lagos accounts for 46 per cent of all electricity used in commerce and industry; 50 per cent of electricity used for domestic purposes; 38 per cent of all drivers' licenses issued; 56 per cent of all telephone calls; 7 out of 19 hotels; 18 out of 19 periodicals; and 4 out of 20 daily newspapers in Nigeria. The fact that the modern sector of the Nigerian economy is highly concentrated in Lagos and a few other large urban areas underscores the close relationship between improvement of urban infrastructure and the pace of economic development.

There are no comprehensive and recent data on the occupational breakdown of employment in Lagos. In a sample survey of central Lagos Island, which includes predominantly persons born in Lagos, Peter Marris found the following occupational breakdown, from which the importance of small-scale trading is evident:

	Men (%)	Women (%)
Clerical	18	1
Skilled manual	30	2
Laboring	13	-
Trading	26	87
Business	3	-
Professional	2	1
Native doctors and priests	3	1
Not working	5	8
	100%	100%

The Ikeja Division includes most of the Western Region portion of the Lagos metropolitan area, excluding only Ajegunle and Ajeromi, which are in Badagry Division. It also includes considerable territory outside the metropolitan area, but this is sparsely populated and mainly agricultural; most of the residents of this territory fall into the agriculture occupational category. The census of 1952 showed the following occupational breakdown for the city and Ikeja Division of the Western Region:

| | Lagos | | Ikeja Division | |
	Men %	Women %	Men %	Women %
Agriculture and fishing	5 (4,000)	8 (3,000)	39 (14,000)	46 (13,000)
Crafts	13 (11,000)	--	14 (5,000)	--
Trading and clerical	25 (11,000)	92 (33,000)	14 (5,000)	54 (15,000)
Administrative, technical, and professional	19 (16,000)	--	14 (5,000)	--
Other (including unskilled and skilled labor)	38 (32,000)	--	19 (7,000)	--

A United Nations survey team[2] in Lagos in 1965 made
a tentative estimate of unemployment in the metropolitan area
of 100,000 persons. In that year, only about 10,000 unemployed persons were registered with the Ministry of Labor
employment exchanges in Lagos and in the Ikeja and Badagry
divisions of the Western Region, but this figure is generally
acknowledged to represent only a small part of true unemployment. The city alone accounted for almost one-quarter
of the nationally registered unemployed. Thus, while Lagos
dominates the wage earning scene in Nigeria, it also dominates in unemployment within the wage earning sector. This
is the result of population seeking to transfer into the urban
wage earning sector of the economy faster than the development of skills in the labor force and than the growth of unskilled jobs. The problem is mainly one of structural unemployment; the unskilled dominate the unemployed, while many
jobs requiring training and specialized education are vacant.
The highest rate of unemployment is among graduates of primary schools. Persons of lower level educational attainment
are not attempting to join the urban economy in as large numbers. By 1960, there were roughly 1,500 graduates of primary school per year entering the work force in the city itself.

The only government bodies directly concerned with problems of employment in Lagos are the Ministry of Labor and Social Welfare and the National Manpower Board. The labor exchange offices of the ministry register the unemployed and attempt to help them find jobs; at the same time they collect industrial and economic statistics. The National Manpower Board is concerned primarily with developing resources for professional and technical manpower for high-level jobs.

The data on income in Lagos in particular and in Nigeria in general are extremely scanty, but it is clear that the preponderant majority earns less than $600 a year. The Marris survey of 110 households heads in central Lagos found the following ranges:

Monthly Income (Ł)	Men (%)	Women (%)
0 - 5	7	20
6 - 10	26	28
11 - 20	36	40
21 - 30	19	4
31 - 40	2	4
41+	9	4

These incomes are high in relation to incomes throughout the country. A federal study commission, the Morgan Commission, made recommendations to the government in 1964 as to minimum wages of junior employees of both government and private establishments. The minimum monthly wage proposed for the Lagos urban area was Ł12, as compared with Ł10 for most other urban areas, and Ł6 to Ł8 for the remaining sections of the nation.

These minimum-wage scales are in effect at present for the majority of persons in wage employment in Lagos. Many employees, however, earn in excess of these levels with the result that the average per capita income (employed population only) is slightly higher than the minimum wage, although many employees receive less than the minimum wage. The average figures exclude those persons who are not in wage employment.

Lagos is very well situated to continue to obtain a large share of Nigerian economic development if its infrastructure is improved. Its port facilities are unequaled, and it is a terminus of the railroad and major road routes to the interior. Industrial parks are being developed in Apapa, by the federal government, and in Ikeja, by the Western Region government. The increasing importance of government and public corporations, many of which have headquarters in Lagos, will reinforce its leadership. In 1960, public establishments accounted for over half of all employment in Nigeria in establishments of ten employees or more, as the following figures show:

	September, 1960 Employed Persons
Federal government	54,700
Regional government	83,900
Local governments	95,100
Public corporations	73,800
Private commercial firms	212,200
Voluntary agencies	34,500
Total	554,200

Source: Ministry of Labor

National economic policy calls for development of a mixed economy with a growing public sector. The National Development Plan, 1962-68, estimates that two-thirds of gross investment in the period will be in the public sector. In the past, about one-third has been in the public sector.

POLITICAL CHARACTERISTICS

Party formation and competition has dominated Nigeria's political history during progress toward indepedence and the six years of its national life. The national parties are directly and intensively involved in local, as well as regional and federal, administration in the Lagos urban area. The history of Nigerian party coalitions is extremely complex; only the highlights are given here.

At independence in 1960, there were three major political parties in Nigeria, each of which had an ethnic and

territorial base corresponding to one of the three regions of
the federation.   Party formation and political conflict in Nigeria have been largely influenced by the division of the country into at first three, and at present four, regions, each of
which is dominated by a majority tribe or related groups.
The Northern Region, within which the Fulani-Hausa peoples
and Moslem religion predominate, is larger than the other
three regions put together.   The Northern People's Congress
(NPC) was created as a political party in 1959, out of a
Hausa-Moslem cultural organization.   The NPC, a well-dis-
ciplined and cohesive party, was led until 1966 by Sir Ahamadu Bello, a traditional leader and descendant of the leg-
endary Muslim reformer Usman Dan Fodio, who established
the emirate system in the Northern Region.   Sir Ahamadu
Bello was premier of the Northern Region.   The deputy
leader of the NPC was Sir Tafawa Balewa, Prime Minister
of Nigeria until 1966. * Since independence in 1960, the NPC
has been the controlling party in coalitions that ran the
federal government.

The National Council of Nigerian Citizens (NCNC) was
formed in 1947 on the basis of a federation of tribal unions,
labor unions, student organizations, and other associations,
with the purpose of achieving independence for Nigeria.   Although organized throughout the southern region, the NCNC
has been dominated by the Ibo tribe from the Eastern Region.
During the preindependence period, led by Herbert Macauley
and Dr. Nnamdi Azikiwe, the NCNC symbolized Nigerian
nationalism.

The third major party at independence was the
Action Group, which was led by Chief Obafemi Awolowo and
forged out of Yoruba cultural associations from the Western
Region.

While there have been shades of policy differences between parties (for example, the NPC has tended to be pro-
Western and economically conservative, while the platforms
of the NCNC have tended to be more populist on domestic issues and neutralist in international orientation), the major

----

* Both Sir Ahamadu Bello and Sir Tafawa Balewa were killed
in the coup of February, 1966.

cleavage among them has been ethnic and regional. Since independence, the NPC has controlled the regional government
of the Northern Region while the NCNC has controlled the regional government of the Eastern Region.

The Action Group controlled the government of the
Western Region until 1962, when conflict within that party resulted in the creation of a splinter group led by Chief Samuel
Akintola, which formed the United People's Party (UPP). A
clash between the two groups in the regional assembly produced the political "crisis" of 1962, under which the regional
government was suspended temporarily by the federal government. Chief Awolowo, leader of the Action Group and
leader of the opposition in the federal government, was shortly
thereafter jailed for treason. In 1963, UPP merged with a
minority party to create the Nigerian National Democratic
Party (NNDP), which controlled the Western Region until
1965, when popular opposition to it contributed to the demise
of the First Republic of Nigeria. Based entirely in the west
and contending that the NCNC was Ibo-dominated and anti-
Yoruba, the NNDP was nevertheless not broadly supported by
the Yorubas.

In the course of elections, each of these parties has
attempted to develop a following outside its major region;
while the NCNC was fairly successful in attracting adherents
in the west, the Action Group came closest to being a national
party. For the most part, however, each has been the party
of the majority ethnic group in its region of origin and the
party of minority ethnic groups in other regions. *

For the federal elections of 1964, the Nigerian parties formed two coalitions that polarized and intensified

---

* This pattern is demonstrated in the results of the 1959 federal election. The NPC obtained 134 seats in the federal assembly, all from the Northern Region. The NCNC captured
58 seats from the Eastern Region, 21 seats from the Western
Region, and two seats from Lagos. The Action Group won 73
seats, 33 of which were in the Western Region, 25 from the
middle belt of the Northern Region, where various minority
ethnic groups are located, 14 from the Eastern Region, and
one from Lagos. A coalition of the NPC and NCNC took over
the government.

political conflict.   The first coalition was the Nigerian National Alliance (NNA), which had the support of the NPC and the NNDP--in other words, of the ruling party of the Northern Region and the ruling party of the Western Region.   It was opposed by the United Progressive Grand Alliance (UPGA), which was supported by the Action Group--the opposition party of the Western Region--and the NCNC--the controlling party in the Eastern and Midwestern regions.   On the eve of the election, after a campaign rife with sporadic violence and allegations of irregularities in registration and nomination procedures, the UPGA called on its supporters to boycott the voting.   While 80 per cent of the registered voters had voted in 1959, only 20 per cent voted in 1964. There was no polling whatsoever in the Lagos district.   Nigeria entered a political crisis after the elections when the supporters of the UPGA refused to recognize the government of the NNA, which had won an overwhelming majority of seats as a result of the boycott.   President Azikiwe proclaimed just before the election, "I have one piece of advice to give the politicians.   If they have decided to destroy our national unity, then they should summon a round table conference to decide how our national assets should be divided before they seal their doom by satisfying their lust for office."   This outlook was shared by many Nigerians who felt that the parties were intensifying tribal and regional conflict for their own ends.   After the election, President Azikiwe persuaded Prime Minister Balewa to form a coalition government that would include representatives of the UPGA.   This was an extremely uneasy alliance, and political conflict plagued the government, culminating in a coup d'état in 1966, undertaken by army officers.

The underlying issues of the 1964 elections were, first, whether Nigeria was to be controlled by the north or the south (Hausa or Ibo), and, second, Chief Awolowo's imprisonment in the Western Region.   There were no consistent ideological or policy issues in the election.   At the end of 1966, a prohibition on party activities was in effect.

The political system in Nigeria is at present on the brink of either change or collapse.   The second ruling military group to ascend within one year, that under Lt. Col. Yakubu Gowon, has called a constitutional conference for the purpose of finding a solution to the political and constitutional problems of the country.   Only if current interregional

conflicts can be contained and eventually softened by future
reorganization will the opportunity for policy cleavages to
emerge in the competitive political process arise.

Within this framework, political conflict in Lagos has
borne little relationship to urban problems and development
policies, although the opposition party in local government
has expressed criticisms from time to time of general administration.

The parties have been extremely active in local government. It is at the local level that regional elections are
won, and control of the ministries of local government in the
regions is a steppingstone to control of the party and the regional premiership. Nominations for local-government
councils are made by local branches of the national parties.
The national-party organizations extend financial assistance
and advice to their local candidates, and in some cases party
leaders campaign for them. After election, the local councilmen's decisions are subject to the influence of party
leaders. Moreover, the controlling party in the Western Region, for example, has pursued party organizational goals
through the exercise of the minister of local government's
powers to issue directives to local-government advisers, to
disallow local appropriations (for example, an appropriation
for a particular chief's salary), and to dissolve local councils. One of the four district councils in the Lagos urban
area has been under suspension since the political schism in
the Western Region of 1962. Its functions are performed by
an appointed management committee. Local issues such as
schools, roads, and water supply in the urban area are not
raised in campaigns and take second place in the ongoing politics of local government, which are dominated by party
competition.

Different parties dominate different parts of the urban
area, and the dominant parties in local governments within
it have differed from the controlling parties of the national
government (NPC) and of the regional government (NNDP)
that supervise the local authorities. This conflict underlies
the state of intergovernmental relationships in the area, cooperation between local authorities and the regional Ministry of Lands and Housing of the West, so that in town planning efforts have been minimal during periods when different
parties controlled local and regional governments, but

intensive when the same party was in control of both.

The central part of Lagos city, settled by traditional Yoruba groups, has supported the Action Group. The periphery of the urban area to the north, which remains mainly Yoruba territory, is also dominated by the Action Group. The newer migrants in settlements ringing Lagos, which are ethnically heterogeneous, tend to regard their own interests as opposed to those of the Yoruba of central Lagos and the Yoruba portions of the Western Region. The NCNC is strong in Yaba and Ajegunle, for example.

The last local elections in the urban area took place at the height of the political crisis in 1963. The trial of Chief Awolowo dominated the campaign with emotionally charged issues. The Action Group, the NCNC, and the NPC were in competition for the Lagos City Council. Although the Action Group was immobilized as an organized party, house-to-house canvassing (called the "whispering campaign") emphasized the threat to the Yorubas and to the Action Group. This succeeded in giving the Action Group a substantial majority over the NCNC in the Lagos City Council. Some public references were made in the campaign to provision of better bus transport and to market planning, but these issues were entirely suffocated by the national conflict.

During the national campaign of 1964, the relationships between local government in the area—dominated by the Action Group and the NCNC, which were in ad hoc alliance in the UPGA, and their supervising authorities, the national and regional governments—dominated by the NPC and NNDP, which belonged to the NNA, were rife with conflict. There are four major points at which the political characteristics of the metropolis directly impinge upon problems of urban administration. First, the dimensions of political conflict underlie issues of metropolitan organization and adjustment of local government boundaries in Lagos. Second, political issues enter into administrative decisions concerning urban services and development. Third, the history of the formation of both political and governmental leadership in the urban area has influenced the attitudes of the population toward its government. And fourth, because of these attitudes and because national conflict dominates local parties, the opinions of the population relating to urban issues have been expressed through politics of protest, which exert unorganized and intensive pressures, entirely outside of the party structure, upon the government.

The first issue, the question of metropolitan organization, is a pressing one in Lagos, where two major technical-assistance teams in the past five years have recommended different forms of metropolitan-government structure. The administrative issues involved are discussed in Chapter 3, but the feasibility and effectiveness of various solutions are highly contingent upon political factors. Prior to 1954, Lagos was part of the Western Region of Nigeria. At that time the NCNC and the NPC, dominant parties of the Eastern and Northern regions, succeeded in their demands upon the colonial administration to federalize the capital city. Lagos, the islands around it, and the immediate strip of the mainland were cut out of the Western Region and established as a federal territory, comparable to Washington, D. C. The urban complex, however, has far outgrown this boundary and the greatest service deficiencies, as well as available land for improvement and development, are situated in the portions lying outside federal territory. Since 1959, the status of this portion of the Lagos urban area has been a prominent issue. While the Action Group defended the rights of the Western Region to retain this territory, the NCNC-NPC advanced the view that it should be merged with the principal city and become part of the federal territory. The defensiveness of the Western Region has been intensified by the fact that another chunk of its area was chopped off by the federal government in 1964, when a fourth region of Nigeria, the Midwestern Region, was established. Cutting off further territory--including Ikeja, in which the regional government has invested in housing and industrial parks--would indisputably reduce the region's power and influence. In 1964, however, the NNDP (which wrested control of the Western Region from the Action Group) adopted the Action Group's policy of defending the Western Region's rights over the Lagos urban area, and as the NPC wanted to bring the NNDP into alliance with it, the NPC shifted its position to opposition to federalization of the entire urban area. The NCNC, which broke off from coalition with the NPC in 1964, sought alliance with the Action Group. As a result, in 1965 there was no political grouping actively supporting further federalization of the area in question, because both of the parties that had a natural interest in this goal were allied with other parties that were strongly opposed.

The issue is further complicated by the espousal by indigenous groups in Lagos of separate-region status for the urban area, which would free it from both the federal government and the Western Region. There are two prominent groups representing the interests of the indigenous section of Lagos population: the Lagos State Movement and the Egbe Omo Eko. These organizations are concerned with safeguarding the interest of "pure Lagosians"--those families who have lived in the city for several generations, as distinct from the newcomers. They maintain that Lagosians do not enjoy the benefits that other regions provide their citizens and that the non-Lagosians who have flooded the city compete with them for the few benefits that the federal government provides.

These factors have produced a stalemate on the question of metropolitan organization for Lagos and explain why no action has been taken on the recommendations of the technical assistance teams that were invited to Lagos. The demand for a Lagos state has gained momentum as the present military government of Nigeria seeks to organize a rewriting of the national constitution and a restructuring of the constituent parts of the Nigerian federation.

The second major aspect of the interaction between politics and administration in Lagos is the day-to-day impact of politics on administrative decisions. Because political conflict in Lagos is concerned primarily with the electoral and economic power of persons and groups rather than with the directions of policy on urban issues, there is a very strong tendency for parties and individual local-government councilmen to interfere in detailed decisions taken in the bureaucracy, particularly those dealing with staff appointments and contracts. Further, the private and political interests of councilmen do not check malpractice and malfeasance in the bureaucracy. There has been, rather, a mutual tolerance between councilmen and senior bureaucrats in which they shield one another in a venal game. Other areas have demonstrated that party involvement in local government can give local council policy a certain cohesiveness and, through organized opposition, maintain a political check on local administration. But in Lagos, the behavior of the parties and the patterns of alliance and tolerance eliminates these functions.

Decisions are made in party caucus without the advice of the professional staff of local government, and the chief officers of local government are put in a position of serving the party in power rather than the council as a whole. These problems are compounded by the tendency to use public authority for private gain, particularly in the allocation of contracts and the management of public funds. Many of the professional chief officers both in the City of Lagos, where they form a separate cadre, and in the Western Region, where they are part of a unified local government staff, are high-caliber individuals who are nevertheless subject to intensive pressures not to interfere with existing power patterns. For example, in the district governments of the Western Region portion of the metropolitan area, if a local-government secretary assigned to a particular council enters into conflict with the controlling councilman, the latter can have him transferred through approach to the regional party leadership and regional minister of local government.

The third point is that there is a considerable gap between the population and the leadership in Lagos that is not bridged by the party organizations. Throughout the colonial period, the administration sought, in an effort to modernize society, to change practices that it regarded as undesirable but that were dear to the traditions of the people. While the colonial administration utilized traditional leaders and chiefs in the system of indirect rule, this proved impossible in the Lagos area on account of conflict between the traditional leadership and the colonial administration that persisted for much of the early period. The exercise of governmental power in this circumstance by the civil service, which included foreigners and Nigerians educated in the West, exacerbated sore points that dominated the relationships between the citizenry and government during that period. In large measure, it helped to foster an image of local administration as a leviathan to which one is forced to acquiesce.

The negative attitude toward urban local government as a policeman persists. The electorate does not act as if it can consciously influence the policy of local authorities.

Although members of new elites of Nigeria are products of the large urban centers, even in these centers the bulk of the population feels little in common with them. There is an increasing infusion into the leadership of Nigeria of members of humbler traditional origins who have Western education and are development- and action-oriented. * They are less allied with the traditional structure of leadership than was the leadership in the colonial period.

Thus, the politically active core in Nigeria is a very small portion of the population--less than 1 per cent--with values that differ increasingly from traditional ones in the country. Legislators tend to be lawyers, doctors, teachers, clerks, skilled workers, and artisans. They tend to be young, and for many of them political office is a highly important source of status and income (although in Lagos, most councilmen possess only primary education, some attended secondary schools, and only a few possess professional qualifications). While many leaders express the desire to foster pride in traditional culture, they are standing at crossroads of values where Western ideas frequently gain the right of way.

Moreover, the negative attitudes of the population toward their governments have been reinforced by popular cynicism with respect to the interests of the political officials in private gain. This has given rise to a profound lack of confidence in local and national government as potential sources of action to fulfill welfare and public service needs.

---

* A survey of 156 members of a "national elite" identified by position and press references (118 of them were officeholders and politicians) determined that 102 of them were from humble origins, being sons neither of chiefs nor of elite families of the colonial period. Cf. Hugh and Mabel Smythe, The New Nigerian Elite (Palo Alto: Stanford University Press, 1960).

These attitudes figured in the motivations of the army officers who took over the government of Nigeria in 1966 and
of the several commissions of inquiry that have been probing
Nigerian public life since.

Thus, the citizen of Lagos feels that the political
party does not represent his interests with respect to urban
life and urban development and that his local councilman
represents the political party more than it represents him-
self as constituent. On the other hand, the population of
Lagos is highly organized in groups that aggregate interests
outside the party structure. It is through these groups that
the citizens participate in politics of protest on several
prominent urban issues.

In addition to the tribal unions and the Lagos indigenous associations, there are several major nongovern-
mental organizations that influence decisions in the urban
area. Dominant among these are the market women's association, the trade unions, religious groups, motor vehicle interest groups, and teachers' groups.

To take a prominent example, the market women in
Lagos have been well organized for more than fifty years.
They have units for particular markets and for sectors of
trade (butchers, fish sellers, etc.). Each unit is headed by
an "Iya Lode," a traditional leader or respected older col-
league. Their tendency to organize has been facilitated by
their common interests as well as by their proximity to each
other; and frequently, they protest government actions by a
march, a sit-in, or other means of demonstration. The market women have protested against slum clearance, against
enforcement of prohibition of parking in the streets and en-
croachments of stalls on the sidewalks, and against changes
in market rents.

The Nigerian Trade Union Congress, a confederation
of trade unions throughout Nigeria, cuts across both craft and
industrial categories. With its headquarters at Lagos, it
watches over the interests of wage workers, protesting and
pressuring when and where necessary. The organized trade
unions have grown rapidly since independence and are today
the most powerful interest group in the urban area. In 1964,
after their demand for increased wages was rejected, they
organized a crippling nation-wide strike. They have

influenced decisions concerning transport fares, rents, and building of low-income houses in Lagos.

In addition, the low-income urban dweller in Lagos has for many years voiced his opinion through participation in public rallies and protest meetings. As early as 1895, 5,000 demonstrators were mobilized before Government House in Lagos to protest tax measures. In 1908 and 1917, public rallies were held to successfully oppose raises in water rates. Massive youth rallies and protest meetings were extensively used by the political parties during the movement toward independence in the 1950's. And, in 1964, the political parties utilized groups of unemployed urban youth to engage in political rallies and various campaign activities that bordered on thuggery.

Most of the interest groups in Lagos exert their pressures directly on government and skirt the party structures. This pattern of pressure and protest tends to give great strength to the opinions of particular groups when an issue is raised within their specific ambit of interests.

CONCLUSIONS

The Lagos urban area is growing at a phenomenal rate. While it is the richest area in Nigeria in terms of both private wealth and public services, unemployment and service deficiencies are severe and are growing worse. The United Nations team that studied Lagos in 1962 identified serious problems arising from, or exacerbated by, rapid growth: competition for land; long and inconvenient journeys to work; extremely bad traffic and parking conditions; shortage of housing; scarcity of housing finance; growth of slums; developing health hazards (particularly due to the absence of a sewage system); underdeveloped human resources; and community neglect.

Above all, the basis of the economic development of Lagos is its port, which is managed by the national ports authority. Congestion of port facilities and the harbor and inadequate transportation services linking it to the interior of Nigeria threaten its future.

As different parts of the area are highly specialized in relation to land use, economic functions, income groups, social values, and political affiliations, they are at once highly interdependent in terms of development needs (for housing, transportation, water and sewage, industrial expansion) and highly fragmented in terms of the capacity to develop and agree on complementary and consistent policies.

The demands upon government are expanding even faster than the population in Lagos. Many aspects of life that traditionally lay outside the gambit of government in Nigeria are becoming government responsibilities with rapid urbanization and modernization. For example, the sheer density of urban development in Lagos requires that a protected public water supply and sewage system be extended throughout the area to prevent the development of severe health hazards. As tribal union and extended-family mutual-aid systems weaken, responsibilities of government in the area of welfare services will grow. Traditional systems of land tenure and market allocation of land must be modified by zoning and land-use planning because of specialization of use and density. The new economic activities and job opportunities require manpower training and vocational education, as well as widespread general education, which the government has never directly provided in Nigeria. Many traditional customs, such as street and courtyard maintenance by particular members of family compounds, are not surviving overcrowding and residential heterogeneity. Government must undertake such efforts as health education and street cleaning. Thus, contrary to the older cities in more developed nations, which have difficult enough tasks in planning for service expansion and rational growth patterns, government in Lagos is embarking upon many activities for which it was never organized previously.

All of these factors present government with a difficult task of planning and implementing urban development efficiently while allowing for diversity; of modernizing while nurturing the best aspects of traditional culture; and of resolving conflicts without eliminating democracy.

The institutions of government responsible for these tasks in greater Lagos, their organization and interrelationships, are the central subject of this study. The research on which it was based was conducted through 1965, and while the major political events of 1966 are identified, the analysis focuses on the systems prevailing prior to that year.

Chapter 2 describes the government structures with formal responsibilities in metropolitan Lagos. Chapter 3 outlines the intergovernmental relationships involved in initiating, financing, and carrying out public services and projects. Chapter 4 discusses the types of formal planning that have bearing on Lagos, and Chapter 5 examines the administration of four key services in the urban area. Finally, Chapter 6 summarizes problems and trends in administration for Lagos and draws comparisons with other urban areas examined in the broad research effort of which this study is a component.

NOTES TO CHAPTER 1

1. See Peter Marris, Family and Social Change in an African City (London: Routledge and Kegan Paul, 1961). Marris discovered that nine out of every ten resident homeowners in this section had been born in Lagos.

2. Otto Koenigsberger, et al. , Metropolitan Lagos (New York: United Nations Commissioner for Technical Assistance, 1964).

CHAPTER **2** GOVERNMENTAL
INSTITUTIONS
FOR LAGOS

     The institutions engaged in administration of Lagos
include those of the federal government, which is constitutionally responsible for the government of the city-federal
territory; the Western Region government, which is constitutionally responsible for the rest of the urban area; the
elected Lagos City Council, which was established by the
federal government to undertake local activities in the city;
four district councils, which were established by the Western
Region to undertake local activities in parts of the metropolitan area; and several public corporations and statutory
boards.

     The position of the federal government in the Fed-
eral Territory of Lagos parallels that of regional government throughout the rest of Nigeria, for the regions are
constitutionally responsible for establishing and supervising
local government. The government of the City of Lagos itself is unique, due to its capital status, but the structure of
government in the rest of the metropolitan area is typical of
that throughout the Western Region.

     Local government as presently constituted in Nigeria
is young and its position uncertain. The colonial administration's practice of indirect rule through native authorities gave
rigidity to traditional systems of leadership (actually creating
chieftaincies where there were none). In the decade before
independence, the formal structure of English elected local
councils was superimposed over these systems. A general
expansion of economic and developmental activities on the
part of government has filtered down since independence to
these local authorities although governmental power remains
concentrated at the national and regional levels. It is not
surprising to find many local authorities ill-equipped to
carry out their part, which is to execute small developmental

projects and manage some public services. Intense party
conflict, traditional conservatism, and very limited local
managerial capacities were not significantly altered by the
organizational superstructure built in the 1950's. As a result, local government is one of the major aspects of Nigerian life that are in crisis in 1966.

GOVERNMENT IN NIGERIA

When Nigeria became independent in 1960, it was a
federation of three regions with parliamentary government
at both the federal and regional levels modeled on the British
structure. A fourth, the Midwestern Region, was created in
1964. The Constitution lists matters over which the federal
government is given exclusive jurisdiction as well as concurrent subjects, while residual powers are vested in the regional assemblies. In a state of emergency, however, the
federal Parliament could legislate on any matter, and in certain circumstances it could suspend regional government, as
it did in the Western Region in 1962. Under normal circumstances, the regions have primary responsibility for development projects and administration of most public services.
In January, 1966, the Constitution was suspended and the
federal military government was established under the leadership of Major General Aguiyi-Ironsi. This regime initiated
steps toward the creation of unitary government in Nigeria; it
abolished the regions and unified the civil service. The government of General Aguiyi-Ironsi proved shortlived* and was
superseded in July, 1966, by that of Lt. Col. Yakubu Gowon,
which resuscitated the former federal system, pending consultation with Nigeria's leaders in an effort to create new
constitutional arrangements**

---

* General Ironsi and his Governor of the Western Region
were kidnapped and killed by soldiers in June, 1966.

** General Aguiyi-Ironsi's government was first styled a
federal military government. Under this arrangement, he
was supreme commander of the federal military government
and of the Nigerian army and was assisted by deputies designated as regional military governors. The federal government and Parliament, as well as regional governments,

Many of the problems that underlay the breakdown of the Nigerian federation are attributable to the fact that it was divided into regions that had different ethnic and language majorities. Because the federal government was based upon parliamentary majority, the Northern Region seemed to have built-in control of the country. The House of Representatives, in which major legislative powers were vested, included 312 members elected for a term of up to five years from single-member constituencies based on population. There was universal adult suffrage in the Eastern, Western, and Midwestern regions and adult male suffrage in the Moslem Northern Region. The City of Lagos had four seats in the House of Representatives. The Senate included twelve representatives of each region, nominated by the regional governor and elected by joint sittings of the regional houses, plus four senators from Lagos and four selected by the Nigerian president. The two houses exercised concurrent powers, but money bills originated in the lower house and could be delayed by the Senate only one month. Other bills could be passed without approval of the Senate after six months' delay, with the consent of the president.

The president, elected by Parliament, was chief of state and commander of the armed forces. The prime minister, who was appointed by the president, was the effective chief executive. He was the leader of the majority party or

------

were suspended. The Lagos City Council was also suspended.

Later, a set of decrees transformed the federal military government into the national military government, the regions into "groups of provinces," and the federal and regional civil services into one service.

In addition, Major General Aguiyi-Ironsi instituted commissions of inquiry into several public institutions, including the Electricity Corporation of Nigeria, the Nigeria Railway Commission, and the Lagos City Council. Further, he appointed study committees on several subjects, including constitutional review and unification of national-regional functions.

Lt. Col. Yakubu Gowon's government has undertaken the following steps: (1) release of major political prisoners (including Chief Awolowo); (2) return to the federal arrangement; and (3) a call for a constitutional conference to review the type of political association desired by Nigerian peoples and regions. In 1967, rebellion in the Eastern Region which declared itself the independent nation of Biafra, suspended negotiations.

combination of parties in the House of Representatives and had executive authority over all matters for which Parliament had legislative authority. Other ministers were appointed by the president on advice of the prime minister, and the Council of Ministers was collectively responsible for executive action.

Nigeria has an independent federal judiciary topped by the Supreme Court, which has original jurisdiction with respect to federal-region and interregional disputes; appellate jurisdiction in civil and criminal proceedings; and advisory jurisdiction concerning the power of the president or the regional governors. It also has exercised judicial review over legislation.

The governments of the four regions of Nigeria were similar in structure to that of the federation. Each had a governor whose powers within the region paralleled those of the president. The executive consisted of the premier, who was appointed by the governor and commanded the majority in the regional assembly, and an executive council of ministers. The regional parliaments consisted of a house of assembly and a house of chiefs, the latter giving special representation to traditional Nigerian leaders. The houses of assembly were elected from single-member constituencies for periods not exceeding five years. They had major legislative powers in the region, except that certain bills could only be introduced by a minister. The delaying powers of the houses of chiefs were the same as those of the Senate at the federal level.

The regional executive councils were the principal policy-development organs. Each included the premier and ministers who were collectively responsible to the assembly. The governor of each region had the power to dissolve the two houses and call for new elections.

The systems of local government throughout Nigeria incorporate elements of both British local-council administration and traditional Nigerian native rule. During the colonial period, the British utilized traditional chiefs and their councils under the "native authority system of indirect rule." However, the real repository of power was the resident or the district officer, who was responsible directly to the administration in the capital and supervised and directed the

activities of native authorities. Since 1950, there has been a
gradual transfer of local powers from the native authorities
and district officer to elected local councils. The district officers have been replaced by regionally appointed local-government advisers.

In the Northern Region, traditional local authority
still prevails, embodied in an emir and his council, who
hold inherited offices. While elected councils have been
instituted by some native authorities in this area, the latter
remain tax-collecting and ordinance-passing units with the
exception of Kano, which has a fully elected city council. *

Local government in the Eastern and Western Regions consists of two tiers of councils: local and district.
The council structure is not uniform throughout the Western
Region, but local and district councils have been established
by the regional government as they were needed and as demands for them were generated. The whole region is divided
into divisions (which are larger than districts), but divisional
councils are being abolished, so that divisions, such as
Ikeja and Badagry, which include parts of the Lagos urban
area, are units of regional-government field administration,
and local government will consist of two tiers only—local and
district councils—though for some purposes, the districts are
also used as regional administrative field areas.

The regional law setting up each council defines its
powers and its relationship to higher or lower councils.
Wherever both tiers have been established in a given area,
one council, usually the district council, is the local taxing
authority and the other council is financed by precepting
against the taxing council. The precepts, or budget demands,
are forwarded to the taxing council, which includes these in
its general estimates of expenditures on which tax rates are
based.

---

* The longer life of traditional rule in the Moslem North is
partially explained by the facts that native authority was more
comprehensively organized here and that the educated elite
in the North has to a large degree coincided with the traditional elite.

The grant of powers to various councils varies with the regional government's assessment of the council's capacities and classification.   This flexibility of local-government structure and powers is useful during the period of transition and modernization, and the system is adaptable to urban areas.   For example, the Ibadan District Council has jurisdiction over the existing Ibadan urban complex and considerable surrounding territory.   Within its jurisdiction are the Ibadan City Council and six rural local councils.   Schools, police, and jails are responsibilities of the district.   The regional government is fully empowered to alter such local-government boundaries without local consent.

All of the councils in the Western Region include both directly elected and traditional members, but the chiefs cannot exceed one-third of any council membership.

THE FEDERAL GOVERNMENT IN METROPOLITAN LAGOS

Federal administration is carried out by ministries and their constituent departments, as well as by several statutory corporations loosely responsible to the ministries. There are no formal federal field units throughout the country, as most direct functions that are not provided by public corporations are provided by the regions.

Within the City of Lagos, however, the national ministries have direct policy-making and operating responsibilities.   The Ministry of Lagos Affairs has been responsible for local government in Lagos; land development, housing, and planning; and general coordination of all of the activities of national authorities with respect to the city.   The Ministry of Works has been responsible for major roads in the federal capital, all public buildings, and water supply. *

---

* In 1966, the military government abolished the Ministry of Lagos Affairs and divided its responsibilities between the Ministry of Internal Affairs (supervision of Lagos city government) and the Ministry of Works and Housing (which took over responsibility for land-use control and housing in the capital).

The Ministry of Commerce and Industry is in charge of licensing and industrial siting in Lagos.   The Ministry of Transport and Aviation is responsible for the port, the railways, the airport, and inland waterways.   The Ministry of Education is responsible for all education and training in the city.   The Ministry of Health is responsible for preventive and curative health services.   The Ministry of Finance and Economic Development is responsible for controlling and coordinating capital expenditures in Lagos.   The Ministry of Labor is responsible for employment services, trade unions, cooperative societies, and social welfare in Lagos, and the Ministry of Mines and Power, for electricity.   Finally, the metropolitan police have been controlled by a minister of state, who is not a member of the cabinet but is placed in the prime minister's office.

        Some of these national-government functions with respect to Lagos have been delegated to special corporations or statutory boards responsible to the ministries, and others have been delegated by law to the city government, but the ministries retain ultimate responsibility and policy control. There is a permanent secretary in each ministry who acts as administrative head of its constituent departments as well as chief adviser to the federal government on subjects falling within the province of his ministry.   The permanent secretary reports directly to the politically appointed minister. The department heads within the ministry report to the permanent secretary, while public corporations and statutory boards are subject directly to the minister.

        The Ministry of Lagos Affairs had a triple role with respect to Lagos: direct operating responsibilities in land control, land-use planning, and land allocation; exercise of the government's powers of supervision over the Lagos City Council; and coordination and synchronization of the policies and programs of various federal ministries and institutions that affect Lagos.   The ministry was divided into four major divisions: administration, land development, land registry, and valuations.   The administrative division (which has been transferred to the Ministry of Internal Affairs) carried out both the supervisory and the coordinating functions with respect to Lagos.   It was charged with all matters relating to the Lagos City Council and to special corporations and boards within Lagos, such as the Lagos Executive Development Board and the Lagos City Transport Service.

This division exercised the government's powers of approval
over Lagos City Council activities. The ministerial concentration of several major activities with respect to Lagos was
reduced in 1966, however, by transference of land and housing responsibilities, including supervision of the Lagos Executive Development Board, to the Ministry of Works and
Housing.

The land division managed government properties
and acquired sites for all national-government activities in
Lagos. It attempted to coordinate and fulfill the demand for
land of various public programs, including those of the Lagos
Executive Development Board. The land registry division
registered titles in the federal capital, a rapidly growing
task as most titles were not registered in the past and are
difficult to establish on the basis of traditional family tenure
patterns. Between 1935 and 1960, the registry dealt with
3,500 title registrations, while between 1960 and 1963 it
dealt with 5,575 titles. The valuation division is responsible
for the assessment of private properties for both local tax-
ation and acquisition purposes.

In addition to the ministries, several public corporations that operate throughout the nation provide public services in Lagos. For example, the Nigeria Ports Authority
and the Nigerian Railway Corporation, both of which are
responsible to the minister of transport and aviation, manage the port and provide railway services, respectively.
Thus, the management and development of the port, which
is the most important economic base for the development of
Lagos, is cut off from both local and direct ministerial authority. Similarly, the Electricity Corporation of Nigeria
provides power in Lagos, as elsewhere. These corporations, which are run by federally appointed boards of directors, tend to be independent in their operations. While
they were created for the purpose of executing projects
initiated by the ministries, their governing boards attained
a high degree of autonomous power. They have independent
operating budgets but receive capital subsidies from the
federal government. During 1966, several of them were
subject to investigations concerning corruption and mismanagement; their boards are to be reconstituted.

THE REGIONAL GOVERNMENT IN LAGOS

Like the federal government, the government of the Western Region of Nigeria, with its capital at Ibadan, is conducted by ministries, each of which is headed by a politically appointed minister and a permanent secretary. Nearly half of the population of the Lagos metropolitan area lies outside the federal territory and is subject to this government. The Western Region Ministries of Economic Planning and Community Development, Local Government, Lands and Housing, Trade and Industry, Transport and Work, Labor, Education, and Health and Social Welfare are directly involved in the development and administration in the Western Region portion of Greater Lagos, and supervise the activities that have been delegated to local government. Various ministry departments implement projects in the urban area, either from headquarters in Ibadan or through division or district field offices. The Western Nigerian Housing Corporation, which is managed by a board appointed by the regional government and which reports to the Ministry of Lands and Housing, executes public housing projects around Lagos, particularly in Ikeja.

The minister of local government appoints a local-government adviser for each district who supervises the operation of local councils and advises the regional government on matters relating to his district. It is the governor in council, however (in effect the regional premier and executive council of ministers), who establishes district and local councils, changes district boundaries, and defines the council's functions. In general, the regional government exercises similar powers in the portion of the metropolitan area outside the federal territory, as the federal government exercises within the City of Lagos.

LOCAL GOVERNMENT IN THE URBAN AREA

The Lagos City Council

The history of local government in Lagos dates back to October, 1899, when a general sanitary board of nine members was created, with the governor of the Southern Region as chairman. Primarily an advisory body, this board, before its demise in 1904, sponsored many improvement schemes in the township of Lagos. However, the Lagos Municipal Board of Health was created in 1909 to undertake municipal improvements that in the previous five years had been the task of the central administration. Although it had considerable formal powers and functions, the Municipal Board of Health functioned for seven years without any permanent staff of its own.

The first representative local government was established in Lagos in 1917 with the passage of the Townships Ordinance (providing for first-, second-, and third-class townships, of which Lagos alone belonged to the first). This provided Lagos with a council, of which the membership varied between six and twelve, as the governor directed. Members of this council were of two classes: Three members were elected for three years to represent the three wards into which the town was divided; and remaining members were appointed or nominated by the government. This arrangement was only slightly modified in 1923, when provisions were made for limited representative membership.

However, between 1940 and 1950, the Constitution and the power of the council were drastically changed. In 1941, the council was authorized to levy property taxes (rates) for township purposes, and in 1950 it was granted a greater measure of self-government, an entirely elected membership, and the post of mayor. *

Changes in political structure in Nigeria leading to federalism brought about considerable fluctuation in the constitutional status of the town of Lagos as well as in the powers of its council. With the establishment of the Western Region and the absorption of Lagos into it, the local government of Lagos was subject to regional control. Further, the Lagos Local Government Law of 1953 (W. R. No. 4 of 1953) abolished the office of mayor, formally provided for the participation of traditional chiefs in the town council, and

---

* The Lagos Local Government Ordinance, 1950 (No. 17 of 1950) which increased the duties and powers of the Lagos Town Council, was based on the English Local Government Act of 1933.

established the Oba of Lagos (a leading chief of indigenous
peoples of Lagos Island) as president of the council with a
remuneration of ₤1,800. However, this general arrangement
was shortlived. In 1954, Lagos was removed from the
Western Region; it was reconstituted into a federal territory
under the Lagos Local Government Act of 1959 (No. 18 of
1959).

The Federal Territory of Lagos, which was accorded
city status in 1963, has since operated its local government
under this federal ordinance of 1959. Local authority is
vested in a city council consisting of 47 members: 42 elected
members and 5 traditional members. The elected members
come from single-member constituencies, while 4 traditional
members are selected from the chiefs of Lagos. The Oba
of Lagos is a nonvoting ex officio member and president of
the council. His main function is to represent the city on
ceremonial and social occasions. The chairman of the city
council, the leading member of the majority party, is political head of the council and of the local authority generally.
There is no separate or specific executive organ in the city's
structure.

Elections to the Lagos City Council are held every
three years with universal adult suffrage. The electoral
wards vary considerably in population (some have as many
as 36,000 people, while others have as few as 7,900).
These wards were defined in 1959 to take the place of the
multimember wards that were utilized previously. Considerable administrative difficulties had been encountered during
the 1957 elections to the Lagos Town Council because of the
multimember wards system. As presently constituted, some
of the smaller wards, which encompass 1,000 to 1,500 families, are neighborhood units that could be effectively organized for community activities such as playgrounds, primary
schools, and libraries. At present, however, they are used
only for election purposes and the relationship between a
councilor and his constituency is attenuated.

The council has organized committees on various
subjects of council responsibility, including: education and
library; estates and general purposes; public health; markets,
parks, and cemetaries; roads, drains, and plans; personnel;
finance; and contracts. (See Chart 1) Motivated by political
interests, it is common practice for members who do not

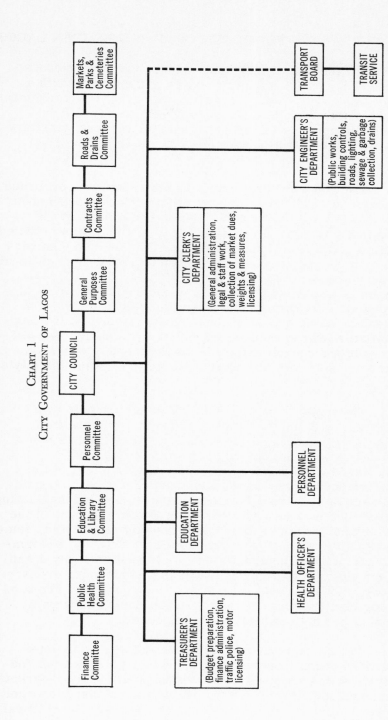

CHART 1
CITY GOVERNMENT OF LAGOS

Finance Committee

Public Health Committee

Education & Library Committee

Personnel Committee

CITY COUNCIL

General Purposes Committee

Contracts Committee

Roads & Drains Committee

Markets, Parks & Cemeteries Committee

TREASURER'S DEPARTMENT
(Budget preparation, finance administration, traffic police, motor licensing)

EDUCATION DEPARTMENT

PERSONNEL DEPARTMENT

HEALTH OFFICER'S DEPARTMENT

CITY CLERK'S DEPARTMENT
(General administration, legal & staff work, collection of market dues, weights & measures, licensing)

CITY ENGINEER'S DEPARTMENT
(Public works, building controls, roads, lighting, sewage & garbage collection, drains)

TRANSPORT BOARD

TRANSIT SERVICE

43

belong to a particular committee to attend and speak at its meetings. As a result, committee meetings become as cumbersome arenas of debate as the whole council and lose the advantages of small working groups. Because no powers have been delegated to them, the committees must burden the full council with a great volume of detailed material; for example, lists of books that the library committee proposes to buy are circulated to all members of the council. *

The responsibilities of the Lagos City Council are to manage those resources of the city that are entrusted to it by national ordinance and to carry out the policies of the federal government in Lagos. It is both a local government and an implementor of federal programs. The functions assigned to it include road maintenance, management of primary schools, traffic regulation, libraries, sewage and garbage disposal, limited public health activities, sanitation regulation, markets, and building control. **

The Lagos City Council owns the Lagos City Transport Service (LCTS), which provides bus transport in the urban area. And, as agent for the federal government, the council administers commercial and motor vehicle licensing.

The city council has no discretionary legal powers to levy taxes. It is authorized to collect tax rates on property

---

* Two British local-government experts who were invited to Lagos in 1963 to comment on the operations of the town council suggested that the committee system would be of greater usefulness if meetings were restricted to committee members and minor powers were delegated to them. G. C. Jones and B. K. Lucas, Report on The Administration of Lagos Town Council, (Lagos: Lagos Town Council, 1963). The present study finds good reason to concur with that suggestion.

** The major categories of expenditure by the Lagos City Council, broken down by council committees, were, in 1964-65 as follows: (1) roads, drains, and plans (including refuse and night soil collection)--32 per cent of the estimates; (2) education--27 per cent of the estimates; (3) public health--18 per cent of the estimates.

with the approval of the Nigerian president in council (in
effect, the minister of Lagos affairs). It is bound by statute
to submit to the president every December estimates of revenue and expenditure for the impending year. Only after
these estimates have been approved can tax rates based on
them be levied and collected, usually well into the fiscal
year. Property assessments are made by the valuation division, in the Ministry of Lagos Affairs. Any council regulations or capital borrowing for projects within its powers
must have prior approval of the ministry.

Considerable problems have been encountered in tax
collection in the city. On October 1, 1960, there were some
Ŀ191,000 in rate arrears; by October 1, 1962, these arrears
had grown to Ŀ345,000. The staff assigned to this task is
limited in both numbers and training, and the job is complicated by the fact that land titles are not clear and communications are rudimentary. Legal action on arrears takes considerable time, as the service of summons is difficult, the
city registrar tends to be overburdened with work, and action
in the normally busy courts is required.

Lagos City Council responsibilities are carried out
by an administration consisting of seven departments and
5,000 employees, including night soil collectors, bus drivers, and street sweepers. The principal administrative
officers are the city clerk, the city treasurer, the medical
officer, the city engineer, the personnel officer, the chief
education officer, and the general manager of the transit
service.

The personnel of the Lagos City Council form a separate civil service cadre, for which the general regulations
are established by the national government. Recruitment and
training of junior employees is the responsibility of the personnel officer in the city personnel ("establishment") department, which also sets salaries according to categories established by the national government. Recruitment to posts
with maximum salaries of Ŀ800 or more requires approval
of the minister of Lagos affairs (after 1966, of the minister
of internal affairs).

While the city clerk is the chief administrative officer, the city treasurer also has important executive duties,
particularly in the budget process. His department prepares

the annual budget estimates on the basis of submissions from
other department heads.   The draft budget is then submitted
to the council committees and the full council for vote before
it is forwarded to the minister.

Together with the city clerk, the treasurer drafts a
preface to the budget, which is a general policy guide for the
coming year.   It summarizes past activities, identifies administrative and financial problems, and outlines improvement proposals.

The senior officers of the city government have high
formal qualifications (as required by law); in most cases,
they have been trained in the United Kingdom.   Their performance is adversely affected, however, by several factors.

First and foremost, city councilmen intervene frequently in the operating decisions of the administrative departments, particularly those dealing with staff appointments, contracts, and prosecutions for law enfringements--
a procedure that has supported favoritism, mismanagement,
and illegal use of public funds.   The activities of the professional chief officers of government are defined by policies
set by the entire council, but they are then subject to continuing intervention or protection in specific cases by individual council members without a mediating executive.   On
the other hand, the committees of the council and the full
council itself seldom consult the chief officers for background
information on policy questions.

Second, there is a shortage of supporting staff and
middle-level employees.   Vacancies are found in the medical
staff, the health inspectorate, the posts of engineers, and
supervisory positions.   The national government has refused
to sanction higher pay scales for Lagos civil servants, and in
some cases, there are no applicants for advertised professional posts in city government.

The third problem is one of logistics, as most of the
city departments operate in extremely crowded office space
with minimal facilities.   In 1964, the city council decided to
build a new city hall, for which acquisition of land by central
authorities has been proceeding.

Fourth, the division of functions among the city departments has been somewhat haphazard. The town clerk's department, for example, is responsible for collection of market dues, while the traffic police, a separate cadre of the metropolitan police, operate out of the treasury department. The town clerk's department also carries out inspection of weights and measures, and licensing. The city engineer's department is responsible for building controls, refuse collection and conservancy, maintenance of roads and drains, as well as public lavatories and street lighting. The education department manages five city schools and supervises other primary schools, most of which are private. The health department operates a midwife service, several medical clinics, immunization programs, and environmental sanitation inspection.

Finally, the city administration encounters public resistance to law enforcement, particularly in traffic control, street and market maintenance, and environmental sanitation. The negative attitude of the citizenry toward local government and the uneven enforcement efforts of local authorities have been mutually reinforcing.

Jones and Lucas, who visited Lagos in 1963, made several recommendations for improvement in city administration. [1] They proposed that there be a review of the division of functions among the departments of city government. They supported enlargement and upgrading of staff engaged in enforcement, inspection, and supervision of the city employees, which developments they felt were contingent upon increased government salaries. Staff supervision and discipline, as well as day-to-day administrative decisions, they urged, should be the responsibility of the professional officers of city government without continuing interference of councilmen. Moreover, they recommended that there be regular discussion between the chairmen of council committees and the chief officers of city government before committee meetings.

These recommendations appear to have merit, but it is unlikely that the underlying political problems of Lagos city government would be altered by minor structural changes. The Lagos City Council was suspended in 1966 and a military administrator appointed for the city. Current investigations by the government are revealing systematic patterns of political and ethnic favoritism, patronage, and bribery that have not been consistent with economic management of local public services.

District Councils

There are four local-government units outside the Lagos city limits but within the metropolitan area. All of them are general-purpose district councils established by the Western Region: in Ikeja Division--the Ikeja District Council, the Agege District Council, and the Mushin District Council; and in Badagry Division--the Ajeromi-Ajegunle District Council. These councils have from twenty to thirty-two members elected from single-member constituencies. With minor exceptions, all seats are contested by two or more candidates. These units were established in the 1950's and have not been altered from the time when the area was entirely rural. There are no lower-tier local councils within these districts (although there are four local councils in other parts of the Ikeja Division outside the metropolitan area). One of the four district councils was replaced--under suspension by the Western Region government--by a temporary management committee appointed by the minister of local government in 1962. (Suspensions of local governments in the Western Region have been fairly frequent since the political crisis of 1962. In 1966, many of the district and local councils throughout the region were being replaced by administrators under the military government.)

The district councils meet at least four times a year and elect annually a chairman, who is the political head of the district authority. Their committees undertake legislative work preliminary to council decisions, but do not have substantial delegated powers. The councils are required by law to appoint finance committees, however, with special functions of administrative supervision, including approval of all agency expenditures of more than Ŀ50.

The Western Region has a unified local-government personnel system, which embraces all senior officers (secretaries, treasurers, department heads, and other staff in posts paying Ŀ300 or more per year) employed by local and district councils throughout the region. Appointments to these posts are made by the Local Government Service

Board, consisting of four members who are appointed by the
regional governor. The board also is responsible for promo-
tions, transfers, and disciplinary control.* Personnel regulations are promulgated by the minister of local government.
The district council itself hires and dismisses lower-level
employees. Appointment by each council of a secretary and
a treasurer is mandatory. Like the Lagos city government,
local authorities in the Western Region do not include an executive official or board per se. The councils are responsible for management as well as for legislation. In the Western Region, however, the secretary is a career officer who
is designated chief administrative officer responsible for coordinating the work of the local authority and advising the
council. He has slightly greater power over other senior officers than the Lagos town clerk.

The four district councils in the Lagos metropolitan
area have been granted a wide range of formal powers. They
are authorized to engage in trade, commerce, or industry.
They are empowered to provide, singly or jointly with other
councils, a variety of works and services, many of which are
rurally oriented. These include: improvement and protection
of agriculture and livestock; schemes for rural development
and settlement; prevention of soil erosion; weights and measures control; markets; hospitals and clinics; drains and sewage systems; refuse and night-soil disposal; public water
supply; public slaughter houses; abatement of nuisances;
cemetaries; housing and urban developments; fire fighting;
public roads, bridges, and paths; street lighting; parking
spaces; transport services; recreation facilities; libraries
and entertainments; welfare services for the young; institutions for the aged or infirm; and community facilities. Of
these, the maintenance of roads, bridges, and paths is oblig-
atory according to the directives of the minister of local

---

* This system reportedly has reduced the incidence of political influence over staff appointments and staff decisions, but
the evidence for such a trend is not strong. Technical personnel are at least occasionally transferred from local units for
political reasons. In actuality, the system has shifted appointments from the local to the regional political arena. The
career possibilities and mobility in local-government service
are heightened by it, however.

government. In actuality, these district councils have not
undertaken public housing programs, public water supply
programs, or any other major services and capital works of
an urban character, for which they do not have adequate financial resources.

The range of subjects over which the councils have
legislative powers (i. e. , may pass bylaws) is as broad,
including: protection of livestock and natural resources,
regulation of markets, regulation of roads and transport,
zoning, public safety and order, licensing, and regulation of
any work or service provided by the council under other
powers. All of the district bylaws, however, are subject to
approval by the local government adviser or the minister of
local government of the Western Region.

In addition to these powers that are assigned to the
district councils in their charters, other functions are delegated from time to time by Western Region ministries. Such
delegation has taken place in the fields of forestry, public
health, and traffic control. Finally, they undertake specific
duties relating to primary education that are assigned to them
in the education law of the region.

The district councils levy income taxes with the approval of the regional government to cover their annual expenditure estimates. These have proved very difficult for
the local authorities to collect and have not been levied at
rates sufficient to finance major public services. Local
officials and the Western Region Union of Local Authorities
have been urging the regional government to authorize a local
property tax for all councils. (On the other hand, Lagos city
authorities have experienced comparable difficulties with
their property tax.) In addition, recurrent grants are extended by the Region to district councils to cover a percentage of the costs of certain services such as police and road
maintenance.

The capacity of the district councils, which were organized for purposes of local rural administration, to participate in the development of modern urban services and facilities are subject to severe constraints—dearth of trained professional staff, small revenue income, little relevant experience of the councilmen themselves, and above all debilitating
party conflict.

An effective local-government-employee training program is a priority requisite to improvement of urban administration, as is generally the case where the general education system has not caught up with modern needs and where there is neither the time nor the experienced senior staff to allow dependence upon on-the-job training and orderly promotion through the ranks. The Ministry of Local Government of the Western Region has established a six-month training program for local-government staff who have secondary school degrees and five years of experience. The curriculum includes accounting, pertinent legal regulations, office management, and basic economics. This program has held few sessions, to date, however. The Institute of Administration of the University of Ife has offered to assist in reorganizing it. The University of Lagos, through its School of Administration and its proposed urban studies program, may also contribute to this effort, generally.

The legal powers assigned to the councils are adequate to enable them to meet urban problems, should their staff and financial capacities be strengthened. In addition, the regional government has full powers to adapt the councils to urban growth. For example, the three councils in the Ikeja Division portion of the metropolitan area could be amalgamated into one urban district, perhaps with constituent local councils to perform selected activities, by unilateral action of the government. There would be political restraints, of course, for which the functions of the lower tier councils might have important ramifications, for the local settlements in this part of the urban area vary tremendously in life style and incomes, as was noted in Chapter 1.

In summary, policy responsibility for the Lagos metropolitan area is divided between the federal government and the Western Region, while operating functions are assigned to five local authorities and several national and regional ministries and statutory corporations. Operating management of existing programs is affected by intense politicization of the details of administration; and capacities for producing expanded urban services and development programs by existing institutions are limited. In the opinion of many of the local leaders, as well as visiting consultants, a major problem of Lagos government is lack of institutional mechanisms for initiating and executing comprehensive development programs for the urban area and for stimulating ongoing cooperation and coordination between the federal and regional sectors of the area. The greatest service deficiencies are in the Western Region portion, where the local governments are not capable of significantly reducing them. Moreover, a rational improvement in housing, land-use patterns, transportation, sewage, water supply, and manpower management will require constant and comprehensive interaction between the regional and federal governments. While the federal government has had a special agency interested in Lagos, the Ministry of Lagos Affairs, this was dismantled in 1966, and there is no Western Region authority with particular interest in the metropolitan area. The question of a metropolitan organization for Lagos has been much discussed in the past five years and has been a key issue of intergovernmental relationships.

NOTE TO CHAPTER 2

1.   G. C. Jones and B. Keith Lucas, Report on the
Administration of the Lagos Town Council (Lagos: Lagos
Town Council, 1963).

CHAPTER **3** INTERGOVERNMENTAL
RELATIONSHIPS

Higher government--both federal and regional--has
dominated urban services and development in Lagos and
other urban areas of Nigeria. Major works and services
are directly provided by these governments or their stat-
uatory corporations, and local authorities not only derive
their existence and powers from them, but also are subject to close control by them. As the people in the city do
not seem to consider the elected local government as primarily responsive to and representative of it, little citizen pressure has been exerted to expand local powers.

In spite of the fact that power is concentrated in the
federal and regional governments, there has been little concerted metropolitan action on the part of the two segments of
the urban area. Proposals for major reorganization on a
metropolitan scale are politically stalemated, and there has
been no initiative taken for joint metropolitan planning or
development projects. That this situation is a deterrent to
significant improvements in urban infrastructure is widely
recognized.

Underlying these governmental relationships is intensive conflict between those interests in the Western Region that not only oppose federalization of the portions of
greater Lagos outside the present boundaries of the federal
territory but argue that all of Lagos should be returned to
the Western Region, and those interests within the federal
government and in parts of the metropolis who want to extend
the federal boundaries to encompass Ikeja, where the Western Region has concentrated much of its investment in both
public facilities and industrial-commercial development.
The particular party alliances for the elections of 1964 re-
pressed this conflict during the campaign, as was noted in
Chapter 1. It is very much alive today, however, and is one

aspect of the larger regional and ethnic issues around which present events and the future of the Nigerian federation revolve.

ALLOCATION OF POWERS

Urban Services and Governmental Roles

Constitutional responsibility for all public works and services is vested in the federal government for the City of Lagos and in the Western Region for the remainder of the metropolitan area. In practice, public service activities are not so neatly divided between the two. Moreover, total responsibility for whole functional clusters of activity has not been delegated by statute to local authorities in either portion, but rather particular duties have been assigned to them, with the result that several governments are involved in each major category of public activity in Lagos.

Transportation administration in Lagos is divided: The city council manages bus transport, while a statutory corporation reporting to the minister of transport runs the railways. Primary trunk road construction is undertaken by the federal Ministry of Works (throughout Nigeria), while secondary trunk roads are the responsibility of the Western Region. Local street construction, maintenance, and lighting are local authority undertakings in both segments of the urban area. Ferries are controlled by the federal Board of Inland Waterways, and both the port and the airport are federal facilities. Traffic control is exercised by the metropolitan police in the city and by Western Region police and local authorities in the remainder of the area.

Responsibility for water supply and sewage services is also divided. A federal agency undertakes production, storage, and purification of public water supply for the urban area as a whole, as well as distribution to industrial users in the city and bulk distribution outside the city. The Lagos City Council finances distribution of water to domestic users within the city limits, while distribution in the Western Region portion is managed through regional engineers. Although existing public sewage (night-soil collection) and refuse disposal operations are performed exclusively by local authorities both within the federal territory and without, planned construction of a closed sewage system will involve the federal government.

Curative health facilities, such as hospitals, are federal and regional in the main, while the Lagos City Council and the four district councils manage some clinics and implement health education and epidemic control programs.

While the federal and regional governments finance and regulate education, the Lagos City Council coordinates primary school management and operates five schools; the district councils enforce regional policies and regulations with respect to primary schools. Most existing social welfare programs are federal, and the Ministry of Labor and Social Welfare conducts community development programs, family welfare services, probation services, youth services, group social activities, and shelters for the needy.

Administration of justice, fire protection, gas and electricity and public housing are to date provided by higher-government authorities exclusively (statutory corporations, in the last two cases). Markets, playgrounds, parks, cemeteries, slaughterhouses, and local cultural facilities are, on the other hand, local operations.

The greatest actual delegation to local authorities has been for the more routine public service activities. The degree to which higher government has retained urban service responsibilities is not mainly attributable to Lagos' status as federal capital, although this status reinforces the tendency and results in the federal government's doing things done elsewhere by regional government. Many of the activities performed by higher governments in Lagos are performed by them also throughout the Western Region (for example, public housing, highways and roads, ports, airports, railroads, electricity, and hospitals). If we take Ibadan for comparison, the only major undertakings of local authorities there in which local governments in Lagos do not have a comparable role are water supply and police. Moreover, the regional government is currently shifting water supply responsibility from the Ibadan local authorities to a regional water board.

The more important determining factors of local powers in Lagos are that the system of predominantly elected councils is very young and that their financial and manpower resources are severely limited. At present, the district councils in the metropolitan area are engaged in only a small proportion of the activities they are legally empowered to undertake, as has been noted. And, while the Lagos City Council is legally empowered to initiate and finance capital projects for transit and sewage services, it is not able to do so.

As in most urban areas, then, there is specialization within metropolitan Lagos among levels of government from nation to town, according to governmental role--planning, policy-making, capital investment, operating finance, and implementation. Even for those public services that have been assigned to local authorities, innovative or developmental activity—including planning, policy formulation, and capital investment—are primarily federal and regional functions. All major improvement projects are proposed at these levels, and without exception, financing for them is authorized at these levels. For example, two transit proposals for the urban area have been prepared by foreign consultants, under the auspices of the Ministry of Lagos Affairs. The sewage scheme for Lagos and water supply extensions are provided for in the national plan and would be financed by the federal government. Public housing and industrial parks are financed by the regional and federal governments.

Execution of large-scale works is entrusted to ministries and public corporations, while local authorities in the area carry out smaller works such as streets, small bridges, and drains.

The major role of local authorities is that of managing established facilities or services. For example, clinics constructed by the federal government are operated by the Lagos City Council. Local market stall rental and night-soil collection are relatively routine managerial tasks.

Financial Resources

It is evident that the national and regional governments account for a very high proportion of public expenditure in Nigeria, although there are no statistics showing total local government finance. The national development plan estimated that government receipts for 1962 through

1968 will be: Ŀ660. 7 million to the federal government;
Ŀ556. 3 million to regional governments; and Ŀ58 million to
local governments.   These figures are in a ratio of roughly
52:43:5 per cent.

The following figures show federal and regional government general expenditure throughout the nation in 1964:

National-government expenditure	Ŀ116, 143, 000
Appropriations to Regions	46, 642, 000
Net expenditure	69, 501, 000
Regional-governments expenditure	Ŀ 69, 038, 000
Grants to local authorities	2, 711, 000
Net expenditure	66, 327, 000

Between 1959 and 1964 the net revenues retained by
the national government increased faster than regional revenues—by 61 per cent, compared with 47 per cent.   In the
same period, the total revenues (including government
grants) of the Lagos City Council increased by about 325 per
cent, starting from the low base of Ŀ891, 000 in the first
year of the present local-government structure and reaching
Ŀ3, 801, 000 in 1964.

Some 70 per cent of national-government gross revenues in 1964 were derived from customs and excise taxes;
6 per cent from direct taxes on corporate profits and personal
incomes; and 24 per cent from other sources, particularly
proceeds from mining, and postal and telegraph services.

The main source of regional revenues is the statutory
appropriation from federal taxes.   Total federal appropriations to the regions accounted for about 67 per cent of their
revenues in 1964, while regional taxes--mainly export duties,
sales taxes, fees, and personal income taxes--comprised 33
per cent of their revenues.   Federal fiscal control over the
regions is limited, however, in that nearly all the monies
they receive from the federal government are from shared
taxes and are constitutionally due them.   Certain federal
revenues are earmarked by the Constitution to be paid into
the distribution pool account, which must be distributed to

the regions at the end of each quarter in established proportions. The regions have independent budget-making and borrowing powers.

On the other hand, local authorities are highly dependent upon higher government for their revenues. The Lagos
City Council is authorized to levy only one tax: the rates on
real property, which are levied each year on the basis of
approved budget estimates. In the Western Region, local
revenue consists mainly of a share of the regional income
tax, which local authorities are authorized annually to retain,
and of grants from the regional government.

About one half of the revenue of the Lagos City Council
is derived from its property tax rates. In 1964, its revenues
were as follows:

Property tax rates from the public	Ƚ1,356,000
Property tax rates from public corporations	160,000
Sub total	Ƚ1,516,000
General government grants	488,000
Earmarked grants and services charges*	1,797,000
Sub total	Ƚ2,285,000
Total	Ƚ3,801,000

Capital financial resources are almost entirely controlled by the national and regional governments. Borrowing

---

* The bulk of the figure for earmarked grants and service
charges is comprised of special federal grants for particular
works and services. Earmarked federal grants were channeled through the Ministry of Lagos Affairs for all major
council services, including health services; roads, traffic,
and street maintenance; parks; education; and welfare services. Revenue from service charges included Ƚ112,985 net
profits from the municipal transit service.

by local governments requires authorization by the minister
of local government in the Western Region and by the minister of Lagos affairs (henceforth the minister of internal
affairs) in the federal territory. Such authorization has not
been given, and those capital projects that local governments
do undertake, such as small bridges and drains, are financed
partially by government grants and partially by local general
revenues. The capital market in Nigeria is severely restricted and higher-government control and mobilization of
public capital will undoubtedly continue. Foreign financial
assistance as well will be required for proposed large-scale
projects for Lagos such as the second Mainland bridge (which
is being executed with German financial and technical assistance at an estimated cost of more than Ł 6 million).

The very limited financial capacities of local government in Lagos, in contrast to its broader legal responsibilities, may have delayed improvement projects. Formally,
for example, the Lagos City Council is responsible for financing and constructing a sewage system and a transit
system. The federal government shows some reluctance
to allocate sufficient funds for these 'local' purposes, and
the city council does not have them to allocate. Thus,
capability and direct responsibility are separated. It is
clear that if development of urban infrastructure is to be
stepped up, one or more of three alternatives will have to
be chosen. First, the federal government would accept full
responsibility for financing major projects in fields legally
assigned now to the city. Second, the federal government
would authorize the city council to raise loans for federally
approved projects, provided the loans would be repaid within
a specified time period (loan charges to the Lagos City Council would probably have to be paid by the federal government).
Or third, new taxing powers would be granted to the city.

Several study teams in Lagos have recommended the
assignment of additional sources of revenues directly to the
Lagos City Council. Reliance on the property taxes excludes
from tax paying all those who do not own property in the city.
A government study team suggested that the city council be
authorized to levy an income tax. [1] Jones and Lucas recommended a 1 per cent local tax on gross incomes both of residents of Lagos who are not property tax payers and of persons who work in Lagos but live outside it. This tax could

be deducted from wages and collected from employers. It has also been suggested that user charges be increased; for example, gas and motor vehicle taxes presently levied by the federal government could be increased to meet the cost of constructing and maintaining bridges, roads, and side-walks. In addition, sales taxes or general excise taxes for sales transactions beyond the given price minimum have been proposed. Finally, there is an urgent need to improve the efficiency of rate collection and prevent further accrual of arrears. The administration of collection is weak, and annual approval of the rate structure by the Ministry of Lagos Affairs delays collection, a delay that could be re-duced if approval of tax rates were based on forecasts rather than on the actual budget, thus enabling the Lagos City Coun-cil to collect most of the rates before the middle of the fis-cal year.

In the Western Region portion of the area, the local income tax would have to be substantially raised or supple-mented by property or other additional taxes if urban local authorities are to undertake the duties assigned to them.

Ultimately, of course, both the willingness of national and regional authorities to assign greater tax resources to local authorities and the degree to which public service im-provements will result are contingent upon improving the managerial and technical resources of local authorities and modifying political patterns.

CONTROLS BY HIGHER GOVERNMENT

The previous discussion has indicated that from the al-location of legal powers and fiscal resources, federal and re-gional governments have the dominant share. Furthermore, these governments maintain close control over local govern-ments in the exercise and utilization of those powers and rev-enues that have been assigned to them. Experience in Ni-geria has shown that continuing fiscal and administrative con-trol are required, not as much to assure coordination with government policy (the existing controls were not designed for this purpose) as to assure regularity and competency in the context of a very young local-government system and limited educational and training infrastructure. At the same time, it has been demonstrated that intensive formal controls alone achieve neither of these purposes.

Fiscal Controls

The approval of all earmarked grants to local governments involves the power to veto or modify the programs and services for which they are to be utilized. Beyond this, all local-government budgets (the estimates) require government approval before they have official status and before full local taxes can be collected. In the Western Region, the minister of local government can approve or disapprove local budget estimates either in whole or in part. District councils must submit their estimates for the impending year before December 31. The draft estimates are submitted through the local-government advisers to the minister, except in the case of a few councils that have greater financial autonomy and are empowered to send their draft budgets directly to the minister. The budgets must have been previously approved by the local finance committee as well as by the full council. If approval is not received by the district council by the beginning of the fiscal year, it can proceed to levy taxes at a rate to bring in at most 125 per cent of the prior year's revenue and to cover only items approved in a prior budget. The minister can order a local tax levy or require sale of local property if the local government has capital debts that have been unpaid for three months or can suspend local expenditure if sufficient taxes have not been collected.

The minister of Lagos affairs could also require that the budget of the Lagos City Council be altered in whole or in part. If approval of the estimate is not received by the beginning of the fiscal year (which is usually the case), the council may make expenditures only for recurrent items that had been approved in the previous year and that involve no increase. Once the budget has received federal approval, the city government is authorized to reallocate funds among the budget heads, provided that such reallocation does not cause an increase in the expenditure of any one department of more than 25 per cent or Ⱡ5,000, whichever is less, and provided that reallocation is not made to any previously vetoed item.

The federal and regional governments audit the accounts of the Lagos City Council and the four district councils, respectively. Moreover, real estate values on which local rates are to be levied in the city are assessed by the federal government. Approval by the minister of local government in the Western Region is required for the district council to charge fees or user charges for council services, or to enter into contracts involving Ⱡ2,000 or more. Local advisers in the Western Region are empowered to examine council accounts at any time.

Other Controls

In both sections of the urban area, the supervising governments have powers of approval over appointment of senior personnel of local councils. In the Western Region, as has been pointed out, local-government personnel of the middle and higher ranks are members of the Unified Local Government Service and are appointed, transferred, and controlled by the regional Local Government Service Board. All appointments by the Lagos City Council to posts carrying a maximum annual salary of Ⱡ800 or more (the minimum salary in this grade is Ⱡ498) require the specific approval of the minister of internal affairs.

In addition to control over personnel, the supervising governments have considerable regulatory powers. The federal government issues regulations with respect to grant-aided services of the Lagos City Council--in effect, all their major services--and major ordinances of the council require ministerial approval. In the Western Region, all local-government bylaws under powers conferred upon the district councils by the general local-government law must be approved by the minister of local government. Those bylaws passed under specific regional authorization such as the education law must be approved by the appropriate minister--in that case, the minister of education. The approving authority can amend the bylaws passed by the district councils or issue alternative bylaws to the council after appropriate notice. In any case, many of the bylaws adopted by local councils follow model legislation drawn up by the regional government. Specific consent of the minister of local government is required for the district authorities to acquire or dispose of land.

Beyond these specific legal powers, the federal and regional governments have considerable powers of general supervision over local authorities, including right of access to all records and accounts. In the city, these powers have been exercised, like the legal controls previously identified, by the administrative division of the Ministry of Lagos Affairs. The Lagos City Council was placed under tighter supervision in 1954, when the territory was federalized, and at the same time, the post of mayor was eliminated. These changes were designed to rid the Lagos City Council of corruption, on which several commissions of inquiry have commented. [2] Investigations during 1966 indicate, however, that they did not achieve their purposes. * The federal government was empowered to appoint a commission of inquiry into the affairs of the Lagos City Council at any time and to suspend the city council for failure to perform its statutory functions. The military government took both of these actions during 1966.

In practice, the Ministry of Lagos Affairs had exercised extremely detailed control of the activities of the Lagos City Council. Both the United Nations assistance team and Jones and Lucas recommended that some of the controls be relaxed. Jones and Lucas suggested that the ministry exercised overdetailed supervision, thus producing delays, and overlapping and wasted efforts. While it is generally held that the federal government should maintain powers of budget approval and of inspection, it was suggested that approval over appointments could be relinquished except for top officers.

In the Western Region, a local-government adviser, who has replaced the preindependence district officer, has access to district council meetings and books, advises the council, and reports annually to the minister of local government. The minister can delegate his approval powers to the local-government adviser, who is the eyes and ears of the regional government in the district. There is some evidence, however, that local officials have recourse, through political channels, to obtain the transfer of local-government advisers who antagonize them.

The region has ultimate control over the existence of the councils: The governor-in-council can appoint a commission of inquiry into the affairs of local government; can

---

* The report of the Saville Commission of Inquiry, 1966, is not yet released.

appoint a management committee or administrator to take over the functions of a local council that has been derelict in the discharge of its statutory functions (this has been done in at least one case in the urban area); or can order that the regional ministries carry out work, enforce bylaws, or perform council functions in cases of failure by the local authorities to do so. Finally, corruption on the part of local-government officials is a criminal offense actionable in the regional and national courts.

The paradoxical coexistence of overly detailed controls and continuing irregularities in local administration is by no means limited to Lagos. It has appeared in several urban areas examined in the research effort of which this study was a component. In general, detailed controls simply substitute one official's discretion for another. The vital elements of effective net control over legality are judgment, integrity, and political objectivity of the supervising officials. Supervisory powers in Lagos have not been extensively codified. Thus, for example, detailed legal criteria for approval or disapproval of contracts or appointments are not spelled out, leaving wide discretion to the supervising authorities and few guidelines for local officials. Moreover, if approval powers by several authorities extend to each action in public administration, responsibility may become so fragmented and clouded as to facilitate illegal or inefficient procedures.

The failure of continuing controls in Lagos ultimately leads to exercise of last resort powers; that is, the suspension of local authorities. Events of 1966 indicate, however, that some higher-government officials were prone to the same practices as local officials.

METROPOLITAN RELATIONSHIPS

Horizontal intergovernmental relationships in the Lagos metropolitan area have been sparse. Government for the area is structurally fragmented not only among five local governments, but also between two higher governments. There has been little communication on the subject of Lagos between federal and regional agencies, and no comprehensive policies have been developed that could provide a schema for coordinated action by the several governments.

Within the federal government alone, the Ministry of
Lagos Affairs was responsible for synchronizing the policies
of the federal ministries and special agencies (for example,
the Nigerian Building Society and the Lagos Executive Development Board). It had a special role in coordinating demands
for land in Lagos, but even at this scale, coordination proved
difficult. While the ministry had direct powers over the Lagos Executive Development Board, it relied on voluntary
cooperation from other federal agencies, and it was not uncommon for other ministries to disregard the Ministry of
Lagos Affairs in carrying out their activities in the city. In
the interest of improving intrafederal coordination and obtaining cooperation from private interests in Lagos, the National Development Plan (1962-68) proposed that the Ministry
of Lagos Affairs establish a standing committee on Lagos, on
which both government departments and commercial concerns
would be represented, to continuously review and coordinate
proposed projects. Such a committee was not organized,
however, and the Ministry of Lagos Affairs as such was
abolished in 1966.

The federal government has not developed broad
policies with respect to urbanization in general or to the
growth and modernization of Lagos in particular. The two
national policies respecting urbanization that have been
enunciated in the past decade do not provide operational
guidelines for coordinated government action. The first
recognizes a need to curtail migration from rural areas to
the cities of Nigeria and calls for expansion of employment
opportunities in the rural areas. Various schemes such as
farm settlements, rural development projects, and location
of food-processing installations in rural centers have been
launched. The second calls for improvement of urban housing, the conditions of which constitute a major grievance to
the labor unions and the bulk of people in low-income brackets. In 1965, the government created the Ministry of Housing to define housing policies and begin a small-scale low-
income housing program. In 1966, this became the Ministry
of Works and Housing, which took over urban land and housing
responsibilities from the Ministry of Lagos Affairs.

The geographic and functional diffusion of authority in
Lagos has sustained inertia in dealing with the long-range requirements of the urban complex--inertia that is an outgrowth
on the one hand, of the political climate and, on the
other hand, of the structural arrangement under which

no unit is responsible for area-wide issues and the local governments have little influence on policy. The challenges posed by rapid urban growth fall between many governmental stools.

The United Nations team studying Lagos in 1962 concluded that its fundamental problem lay in the deficiency of policy-making mechanisms to cope with large-scale factors of land, housing, transportation, water, and sewage. As long as there are no comprehensive policies on these matters, no operational goals or targets, and no established priorities, governmental action will continue to be slow and piecemeal, and present investment in urban infrastructure will not bring as great a return in long-range improvement of urban life as it might.

Another result of the present structure is significant inequity in the services enjoyed and taxes paid by various sectors of the urban population. There are no housing programs in Mushin and Ajegunle, where they are most needed. Ajegunle receives neither public water supply nor transit services, which are extended to other parts of the urban area. Schools and roads in the Western Region portion are extremely inadequate in comparison to those in the city. And most hospitals and clinics are in the federal territory, too far from the residents of the outer portions of the urban area to benefit them.

Structural fragmentation in the Lagos metropolitan area is reinforced by political conflict (and vice versa) and by the tendencies of each agency and government to act in isolation and to take a defensive attitude toward an outsider's interference. When the federal government called a meeting in 1964 to discuss proposals for reorganization made by the United Nations technical-assistance team, the Western Region delegation did not attend. Both federal and regional agencies tend to regard their project proposals as secret documents; for example, schemes under consideration for a central sewage system in Lagos have not been released to the public, to local governments, or to other interested parties.

At the operating level of urban administration, lack of cooperation frequently raises the cost and reduces the output to the public of government projects and services. A most important problem involves land. The Lagos Executive Development Board (LEDB) requires cheap and plentiful land for low-income housing. Such land is located outside the federal territory, where at present the agency is not legally empowered to act. Therefore, the costs of public housing and land reclamation in Lagos are higher than they need be. At the same time, the programs of the Western Region Housing Corporation in Ikeja are in no way coordinated with those of the LEDB. The routes and operating schedules of buses, ferries, and trains in the area do not complement one another although it is frequently necessary to use more than one mode for a journey to work. An example of difficulties of narrower scope is the attempt by the city officials to prevent vehicles licensed by the Western Region to operate public transportation services in the city in contravention of local traffic and transportation regulations.

The district councils in the Western Region have never utilized joint boards or services although they are entitled to do so. The legal authorization that they may cooperate, however, is meaningless under current circumstances, for the district councils are not equipped to provide the type of services that would benefit by joint management, in any case.

Nevertheless there have been several ad hoc responses to the demands for governmental activities that cross jurisdictional boundaries in the metropolitan area, most of them more fortuitous than planned. A division of the Electricity Company of Nigeria, a federal enterprise, serves most of the urban complex. One Federal Posts and Telegraph division serves both Lagos and Ikeja. The Lagos City Transport Service, an agency of the city council, serves Mushin, Ikeja, Shomolu, Oshodi, and other areas outside the city. Lagos Water Supply, a federal agency, serves areas both under the city council's jurisdiction and under the jurisdiction of the Mushin and Ikeja district councils. Observers of the Ikeja Town Planning Authority sit in on meetings of the Lagos Executive Development Board, but this has not brought about any discernible working relationships between the two agencies. Considerable operating cooperation takes place between the Western Region and city fire-fighting and police activities, two areas in which the needs for cooperation are the most immediately visible and intense.

It is clear, however, that far more intensive relationships between the governments involved (contingent first on resolving their basic conflicts and filling of the policy gaps) are required to increase the efficiency and rate of improvement in urban infrastructure in Lagos.

Two major proposals have been made for governmental reorganization to meet these requirements. The United Nations technical-assistance team proposed the creation of a metropolitan development authority.[3] This study, which was undertaken by a team of consultants under the auspices of the Ministry of Lagos Affairs and the United Nations, assessed the economic and social problems related to the growth of the Lagos urban area and concluded that Lagos should have area-wide administration without modification of existing boundaries between the federal territory and the Western Region. Believing that coordination by one federal ministry could not be effective, the team urged that a metropolitan development agency (MDA) be assigned responsibility for implementation of federal, regional, and local development programs in the urban area and coordination of the activities of various other public agencies (such as Nigeria Ports Authority, railway corporation, electricity corporation, and the Western Region Housing Corporation). The creation of the agency would require concurrent legislation by the federal and regional parliaments. The MDA would jointly be responsible to the federal and Western Region governments and its powers would be clearly circumscribed. Its service area would be larger than the existing urban complex and would be subject to review at intervals of no more than ten years.

The agency would be managed by three full-time board members appointed by the federal prime minister in consultation with the premier of the Western Region. The three board members would be drawn from a list of experienced men prepared by the federal and Western Region public service commissions in joint session and would be salaried officers, appointed for five years or more, with secure tenure of office except for cases of grave misconduct. Decisions of the MDA would be by simple majority and the chairman could refer important issues to the federal government for orders. The chairman would appoint and convene an advisory council consisting of officers of the ministries and departments of both governments concerned, professional officers of the local authorities, and representatives of the statutory corporations and other organizations.

The administration of the MDA would consist of four directorates: a directorate of land and transport, a directorate of housing, a directorate for water supply, and a directorate for drainage and waste disposal. Each of these would be headed by a professionally qualified director, assisted by appropriate technical and administrative staff.

Broad functional responsibilities would be assigned to the MDA:

1. It would be empowered to initiate or to execute development works scheduled in federal or regional development plans.

2. It would be responsible for land-use control and zoning, having power to acquire, to develop, and to distribute land for housing, public services, industry, and other urban needs, in accordance with a general land-use plan.

3. In the transportation field, it would coordinate the planning and design of road projects, bridges, parking facilities, water-transit routes, and rail communications; and it would manage any new rapid transit or other public transport undertakings.

4. It would be the area's major housing authority and would set and try to achieve annual targets of house construction. It would give technical assistance to private home builders; provide mortgage finance, small loans for low-cost housing, and roof loans; and administer programs of aided rehabilitation.

5. It would take over all water-supply services and facilities in the urban area and would be charged with estimating the future water requirements of metropolitan Lagos, constructing supply and distribution facilities, and extending metering.

6. It would assume all responsibilities for waste removal and sewage disposal. It would plan, execute and operate storm water drainage, industrial effluent treatment, and underground sewage systems.

7. Finally, it would sponsor truck farming and market gardening in the metropolitan area.

The powers of the metropolitan development authority to carry out these responsibilities would be broadly defined in the creating statute. They would include authorization to manage public land; to take over assets of specified government agencies; to expand, construct, and operate new facilities; to exercise the right of eminent domain on behalf of the federal or regional governments; to inspect private properties; to enter into contracts; and to determine and collect fees for services rendered. It would adopt its own budget and have authorization to borrow money and issue debentures. It would have power to pass ordinances dealing with the services entrusted to it.

The authority would prepare land use, housing, water and sewage, and transportation plans, as well as a master plan for the metropolitan area. In addition, it would draw up a capital program synchronized with the master plan and with the economic development programs of the federal and regional governments.

Thus, although the proposed authority would be structured like a development corporation, it would have powers approximating those of a full-fledged government jurisdiction. In effect, it would not only act as an implementing agency for government projects, but would have major planning, operating, and regulatory powers. The MDA would assume powers now being exercised by the Lagos Water Supply Agency, the Lagos Executive Development Board, the Western Region Housing Corporation, and the Western Region Town Planning Department, as well as certain responsibilities presently vested in the local governments. It would appear that the operating autonomy of the MDA would exceed that of existing local governments, for it would have independent budget-making power and borrowing capacity.

On the other hand, the MDA would be partially dependent upon government for financial resources. Federal and regional grants and loans would be utilized for major development projects. According to the proposal, its own revenues would include the proceeds from fully self-supporting services, such as water supply, housing, and industrial-site development. It was suggested that user charges for these services cover operating costs and debt service. In addition, it was assumed that improvements resulting from MDA projects would produce increases in the taxable value of properties in the metropolitan district. The net increase in the tax income of the local authorities arising from these improvements would be shared between those authorities and the MDA on the basis of a formula agreed upon prior to the execution of projects. In fact, adjustment of assessments is not likely to be automatic.

The study recognized that the principle of self-support should not be carried to the point of creating inequities or distortions in long-term social and economic needs. It acknowledged that it might be necessary to subsidize low-income housing and truck gardening in the urban area.

The second major proposal for reorganization in Lagos was made by Jones and Lucas, who studied the Lagos City Council under the auspices of the council and the Ministry of Lagos Affairs in 1963. [4]

Jones and Lucas concluded, "We have no doubt at all that a unified local government system for the whole of greater Lagos is necessary." They explicitly rejected the alternative of a second-tier metropolitan government and favored organization of a single area-wide local government on several grounds: It would be a simpler system; it would avoid the expense of duplicating staff and equipment; and the existing Lagos City Council appeared to be capable of taking on new responsibilities provided certain administrative reforms were made. They pointed out that under a two-tier system in Nigeria, one council is normally financed by precepts on the other. They felt there would be conflict between a second-tier metropolitan unit and existing local authorities, who would object to handing over a large part of local revenues. Therefore, Jones and Lucas recommended that a greater Lagos council, directly elected by the people, should be the single local government in the metropolitan area with both planning and administrative responsibilities. Its jurisdiction would be defined by a technical commission.

The boundaries between the federal territory and the Western Region would not be changed even though greater Lagos would span them. The portions of the Western Region that fall within the new municipality would remain for all

other purposes part of the region. For nonmunicipal purposes, the residents of the Western Region portion of greater
Lagos would continue to vote, pay taxes, and owe allegiance
to the regional government. It is implied, however, that the
federal government would be the supervising authority over
the greater Lagos council, exercising less detailed control
than it presently maintains over the Lagos City Council.

The new council would take over the planning functions
of the Lagos Executive Development Board and would be responsible for preparing and enforcing a new master plan and
preparing a development plan for the urban area. The Lagos
Executive Development Board and the Western Region Housing Corporation might continue to undertake site preparation
and house construction, but would hand over houses built to
the council for management and maintenance.

It was further recommended that the council build
public housing, develop recreational facilities, and take over
water supply. Tax resources would be expanded, and the
council would be authorized to borrow for projects approved
by the government.

Although the Jones and Lucas report was accepted
in principle by the Lagos City Council, as was the United Nations report by the Ministry of Lagos Affairs, there were no
active efforts to carry out the reorganizational aspects of
either of these reports. Although both recommendations
avoid changing the boundary between the federal territory
and the Western Region, neither one faced up to the political
conflicts between these two units. The metropolitan development agency proposal would concentrate vast powers in an
authority over which the federal government had ultimate
control. Although the Western Region government is to be
consulted, for example, it is the federal prime minister
who appoints the board members. On the other hand, the
greater Lagos proposal is not clear on the role of the Western Region. Given the very close involvement of the regional government in municipal activities at present, it
would be difficult to define precisely what the "municipal
purposes" would be for which the outlying areas of the Lagos
metropolitan complex, such as Mushin and Ikeja, would be
removed from regional power, and for what purposes they
would remain subject to regional authority. Both proposals
remain stalemated. The urban boundary issue is inextricably

bound up with regional and political conflicts, which came to
a head in 1966, and the demand for "regional" or "state"
status for greater Lagos gained momentum during the 1966
constitutional review (the area of the proposed state spans
the present urban area and beyond).

The fundamental differences between the two proposals are interesting in terms of general organization mechanisms for metropolitan administration. The metropolitan
development authority involves a high concentration of planning and operating functions in an appointed special authority,
while vesting policy control and financial decision-making in
the national government, which would unquestionably be a
serious blow to the development of elected local government.
On the other hand, the tradition of elected local government
is short in Lagos; local authorities to date have not been
granted extensive powers, nor have they engaged the primary loyalties of the population. The MDA proposal mani-
fests a familiar desire to treat urban government functions
in businesslike fashion, supposing that the economic functions of government can be and should be lifted out of the
political arena of representative government and insulated
in a public authority operated according to modern corporate practices. The difficulties with this approach, however,
are manifold; the statutory corporations in Nigeria do not
appear to have a uniformly better record than general government agencies as to maintaining legal, equitable, and
efficient practices. The economic functions of government--
planning and providing major infrastructure and public
services--are by far the most important in the urban context.
If control of these functions and therefore of the fundamental
decisions as to the future of urban form and life is essentially
cut off from general government institutions within the area,
the implications for representative government must be explicitly considered.

The Jones and Lucas proposal would concentrate
greater powers in a large-scale elected government, while
maintaining the rights of the federal government to exercise
supervision and control. It is predicated on the existence of
responsible representative government. It is clear, however,
that if the greater Lagos council were to be an effective metropolitan government, its financial, technical, and staff resources and capabilities would have to be vastly improved.

The judgment that it is capable of taking on new responsibilities appears dubious at best in light of its record.

Both proposals place planning and operating responsibilities within a single organization, although the Jones and Lucas proposal calls for a special committee of the council that would be solely responsible for planning. These arrangements raise two questions: Is the planning function not likely to become focused on the short-run operating needs of the Agency? Are there not likely to be problems of plan implementation unless the federal and regional governments, which control capital resources, are closely involved in the metropolitan development planning process?

In the last analysis, however, neither proposal was politically feasible of implementation, and structural reorganization will not radically alter the underlying political problems in Lagos, which are not merely metropolitan but nationwide and arise from the failure of political leadership to resolve conflicts and to formulate substantive development policies. Moreover, neither reorganization plan strikes at the heart of administrative problems in Lagos--personnel deficiencies, lack of commitment to public service, and weak local council governments with very limited financial resources. Both paralyzing political conflict and administrative weaknesses can thrive within a metropolitan government as well as without it, as other urban areas of the world have illustrated.

NOTES TO CHAPTER 3

1.   Sir John Imrie, Report into the Relationship Between the Federal Government and the Lagos City Council (Lagos: Federal Government Printer, 1959).

2.   Bernard Storey, Report of the Commission of Inquiry into the Administration of the Lagos Town Council (Lagos: Government Printer, 1953); and R. N. Rapson, Report of Commission of Inquiry into Alleged Irregularities in Connection with the Collection of Money and the Allocation of Market Stalls in Respect of Proposed Ereko and Eko-Awo (Lagos: Federal Government Printer, 1959).

3.   Otto Koenigsberger, et al. , Metropolitan Lagos (New York: United Nations Commission for Technical Assistance, 1964).

4.   G. C. Jones and B. Keith Lucas, Report on the Administration of the Lagos Town Council (Lagos: Lagos Town Council, 1963).

CHAPTER PLANNING FOR LAGOS

While there has been no general planning for the Lagos metropolitan area, several plan-related activities impinge upon its development. Within the National Development Plan (1962-68), both the federal and the Western Region programs deal with public investment in Lagos. The Lagos Executive Development Board is responsible for land-use planning for the central city, while a Western Region town planning authority is responsible for land-use planning for Ikeja. Both economic and physical planning efforts have been rudimentary, however, and subordinated to the exigencies of immediate project design.

ECONOMIC PLANNING

Economic planning in Nigeria deals with forecasts and goals for the utilization of investment capital, for the most part. The central planning organ of Nigeria is the Economic Planning Unit, a division of the federal Ministry of Economic Development. Its staff of nine was aided by foreign assistants during preparation of the current six-year development plan. In each of the Nigerian regions, the ministries of economic planning, which similarly have small staffs, are counterparts of the federal unit and together with it are responsible for preparing the National Development Plan which consists of four separate chapters--the federal program and three regional ones. The nature of statistical services and national accounts is rather rudimentary. The Federal Office of Statistics in the Ministry of Economic Planning is headquartered in Lagos and has branches in each of the regions, and the regions are also developing statistical offices. Technical assistance is being utilized to strengthen both the statistical and national accounting services. All of these units have severe shortages of staff and equipment, however, and have met with difficulties in obtaining information from operating departments. It was not possible, therefore, to

establish general macroeconomic targets from which to derive sectoral targets and construct the development plan.
Rather, the starting point for the plan was a collection of
separate projects submitted to the planning units by various
ministries and public corporations. Most of these agencies
do not have internal planning staffs, however, so that economic analysis has played a restricted role in the program
formulation. [1] In the words of the plan document itself,
"The approach to this plan . . . has consisted firstly of
ensuring the economic desirability and feasibility of projects, secondly of coordinating them as to size and timing
to ensure their consistency, and thirdly, of comparing requirements with the availability of resources. "

The federal planning unit analyzed the programs forwarded to it in terms of very general policy instructions
from the Council of Ministers. It negotiated with the various
ministries over the advisibility of suggested projects and
referred conflicts to the federal cabinet.

Simultaneously, a similar procedure was followed
for the current plan in each of the regions. The products of
these efforts--one federal and three regional draft pro-
grams--were submitted to the federal cabinet and regional
executive councils, respectively, for approval.

Subsequently, the federal planning unit studied the
regional programs to ensure compatibility with the federal
program. While it is empowered to recommend the maintenance or rejection of the various regional projects, this did
not prove necessary, since the regional and federal planning
officials had been in regular consultation throughout the technical phases of plan preparation. Should it have been necessary, it would have been extremely difficult for the economic
planning unit to exercise much authority over the regional
programs, as it is merely a subdivision of a relatively young
federal ministry. Any remaining disagreements at this stage
must be resolved by the National Economic Council, which
includes the ministers of finance and economic planning from
the federal and regional governments and is responsible for
coordinating the various development programs and adopting
a final version of the plan.

The council is served by the Joint Planning Committee,
a staff group that consists of the permanent secretaries and

other senior civil servants concerned with economic development from the federal and regional governments.   The Joint
Planning Committee prepares statements on objectives and
advises the National Economic Council both on the compatibility of the various development programs and on the final
form of the national plan.   These tasks are performed at
regular meetings throughout the plan preparation process.

The National Economic Council is the highest responsible planning authority.   After the current six-year development plan was endorsed by the council, it was submitted to
the national Parliament.   Similarly, the regional chapters
of the National Development Plan were submitted to the re-
spective regional parliaments.   The parliamentary majorities approved the plans without amendments, and the ministries of economic development and information undertook
to publicize the plan extensively throughout Nigeria with the
aid of radio, television, and newspaper media.

Planning Projects for Lagos

The Nigerian National Development Plan, then,
essentially identifies a collection of projects that, because
of the nature of plan preparation, are not designed and integrated in terms of precise operational targets and development policies.   Investments relating to the Lagos metropolitan area are found scattered within two chapters of the plan:
the federal program and the Western Region program.

The total projects of the federal program amount to
Ł412,510,000 in capital expenditure for 1962-1968.   Of this,
25.1 per cent is allocated to transport, 23.8 per cent to
electricity, 10.7 per cent to trade and industry, 7.3 per cent
to communications, 7.1 per cent to education, and 5.6 per
cent to town and country planning.   This last category, which
includes expenditure on specified projects and amounts to
Ł23.16 million, is entirely related to the Federal Territory
of Lagos.   This total is divided as follows:

Million Ł

Lagos Executive Development Board, housing, land planning, industrial parks, highway clover leaf	15. 028*
African Staff Housing Fund, housing in Lagos	1. 830
Nigerian Building Society, housing loans	1. 500
Additional federal contribution to housing in Lagos	1. 344
Lagos sewage system	1. 565
Lagos City Council projects (for markets, streets, one bridge, drainage, abattoir)	1. 843
Victoria Beach Protection Survey	. 050
Total	23. 160

Several additional projects for Lagos are included in other sections of the federal plan. For example, under the heading of urban water supplies, Ł1. 8 million is allocated to expand the metropolitan area supply capacity. The rubric of transportation includes construction of a second bridge from Lagos Island to the mainland by the Ministry of Works; port facility expansion by the Nigerian Ports Authority; and railroad improvements.

The program of the federal Ministry of Education calls for a capital expenditure of Ł3. 123 million for primary school construction in Lagos, Ł1. 980 million for secondary

---

* Of which Ł10. 572 million was the Lagos Executive Development Board's own funds.

education in Lagos, and Ł2. 026 million for technical and
teacher training in Lagos. In addition, the University of Lagos is allocated Ł5. 514 million. Of the federal Ministry of
Health's capital programs, totaling Ł10. 304 million, about
Ł7. 5 million will be invested in health institutions primarily serving Lagos.

In addition, Ł488, 000 is allocated to fire-fighting
equipment for Lagos; Ł1 million to a sports stadium;
Ł255, 000 to the Lagos Cooperative Central Financing Society (which provides credit to local fishing, building, and
other cooperatives); and Ł505, 000 to youth and welfare programs.

In total, then, over Ł50 million (well over 10 per
cent of total investment called for in the federal program)
is planned by the federal government for investment in
facilities relating to physical and social infrastructures of
Lagos in the six-year period. Housing programs, alone,
account for about one-third of the planned expenditure in Lagos; education and health are the next largest categories.

Neither design nor cost estimates for the various
projects called for in Lagos are spelled out in the plan. For
example, the figure of Ł1. 6 million for the beginning of a
comprehensive sewage system for the city cannot be evaluated because there is no operational project proposal indicating the type or extent of the system to be constructed.
Neither is it related in any way to figures for expansion of
the water supply system, to which it would have to be ultimately linked. Moreover, there are some discrepancies between the plan and reality--for example, because the plan
assumes that the Lagos slum-clearance program will pay for
itself, no capital resources are allocated to it (in fact, present evidence is that the returns from sale of cleared land
will be far below costs).

The Western Region program within the National Development Plan includes investments by the region, some of
which are to be made within the Lagos metropolitan area.
The projected capital expenditure of the regional program,
amounting to Ł90, 287, 000 (somewhat less than one-quarter
of the magnitude of the federal program), is not broken down
by geographic sectors of the region.

The projects that are identified as falling within components of the Lagos metropolitan area include a 300-acre extension of industrial parks at Ikeja, at a capital cost of Ŀ640,000, and creation of a 500-acre industrial park at Ajeromi, at a capital cost of Ŀ1,347,000. These projects, as well as construction of public housing at Ikeja, will be financed by the Western Nigerian Housing Corporation. The regional program also proposes to invest in water supply facilities to serve industrial parks at Ikeja, Ajeromi, and Mushin. It plans to carry out a town planning effort in Ikeja and to establish fire-fighting services in that town. The regional government will invest in schools, roads, and public health facilities in its portion of the metropolis. Finally, investment by the Western Nigeria Finance Corporation and the Western Nigeria Development Corporation in commercial and industrial enterprises will take place at Ikeja.

TOWN AND COUNTRY PLANNING

Responsibility for land-use mapping and physical planning in the City of Lagos is vested in the Lagos Executive Development Board (LEDB). This multipurpose agency was created by the government in 1928 under the Lagos Town Planning Ordinance (Chap. 95 of the Laws of the Federation of Nigeria) to clear unsanitary buildings, redevelop, and rehouse displaced persons in the area of Oko-Awo after a plague.

The LEDB has since become the planning and housing authority for the Lagos municipal area. Its main activity gained prominence in connection with the Lagos Central Planning Scheme of 1951, which required slum clearance in central Lagos and the subsequent development of the area for commercial activities.

Under the Republic of Nigeria, the LEDB, as a statutory corporation, was directly responsible to the minister of Lagos affairs. It had thirteen members; a chairman, appointed by the minister of Lagos affairs; six ex officio members (the Lagos city clerk, the city engineer, a representative of the federal Ministry of Finance, the harbor master, and two members of the Lagos City Council); three additional appointees of the minister of Lagos affairs; and one representative of the Lagos Chamber of Commerce. The chief executive officer of the Ikeja Town Planning Authority attended meetings of the board as an observer.

Since the federal military government was established in 1966, the LEDB is no longer responsible to the Ministry of Lagos Affairs, which was abolished as such. It is now accountable to the federal Ministry of Works and Housing, which emerged in 1966 under the federal military government and incorporated the former Ministry of Works and Survey and the Ministry of Housing. Its board was reconstituted to consist of the director of the federal Ministry of Works and Housing as Chairman; a secretary appointed by the board; a representative of the Ministry of Finance; the city engineer; the senior city medical officer of health; the chief executive officer of the Ikeja Town Planning Authority; and an officer of the armed forces. Under this new arrangement, the LEDB is an executive agency under the Ministry of Works, with special responsibility for the formulation and implementation of physical plans in the City of Lagos.

The activities of the LEDB, whose jurisdiction is confined to the City of Lagos, include slum clearance, land reclamation, construction of roads and drains, development of housing and industrial parks, and preparation of a master plan. The board exercises limited powers of eminent domain and passes on building applications concurrently with the Lagos City Council (which is a public health and building bylaw authority). While it has some policy-making powers, its major role is to execute federal programs, and its activities (apart from planning and zoning) are financed by federal capital grants and loans, and by revenues from fees, rents, and sales of developed land.

The Lagos Executive Development Board has had fairly consistent relationships with the Lagos City Council, since council members sat on it and the Ministry of Lagos Affairs supervised both institutions. Under the new arrangement, local-government representatives are not included on the board, and supervision of general local government is transferred to the new Ministry of Internal Affairs.

The LEDB administration is headed by a chief executive officer, to whom the division heads report. The divisions include administration and law, town planning, engineering, land survey, finance, architecture, and estate

management. These are headed by chief officers (the board
secretary, the senior town planning officer, the senior engineer, the senior surveyor, the finance officer, the senior
architect, and the senior estate officer, respectively) who
are selected by the board and approved by the minister. Coordination of the various divisions is effected by the chief
executive officer, who holds fortnightly meetings of his division heads.

The planning responsibilities of the Lagos Executive
Development Board have taken a back seat to its operational
responsibilities. There are only three trained town planners
in the agency, and there is no completed general master plan
for the city. Planning activities to date have produced project plans for small parts of the city in which housing, clearance, and land development projects are being carried out.
These small-scale land development programs are prepared
by the LEDB staff, but are ultimately approved, controlled,
and financed by the federal government.

The project-planning process begins when officers of
the LEDB undertake surveys of the area of the city in question, which they forward to the chief executive officer of the
board with technical advice. At this stage, the chief executive officer generally calls a staff conference to examine
proposals and to define program goals. Financial implications and available resources are then considered by the finance division. The chief executive officer presents final
project proposals to the full board, which may accept the
proposal or suggest modification. The board's decision is
subject to the approval of the minister. As capital finance
is provided by the federal government, the federal cabinet
ultimately has decisive powers. The resultant documents
are layouts for development or redevelopment of neighborhoods within Lagos.

The LEDB maintains a master zoning document,
which is utilized as an interim development control; board
projects and all building permit applications are checked
against it. In addition, the LEDB has a housing plan, which
states goals for the private and public sectors respecting
quantity and quality of new housing construction and supports
the slum-clearance program. Finally, the Lagos Executive
Development Board has published a report entitled "Planning
Standards for the City of Lagos," which suggests minimum

standards for schools, housing, and population density. The
report was prepared by the chief executive officer in connection with a training program for town planners in Nigeria and
is based upon statistics provided by the federal Ministry of
Education, the Lagos City Council, the federal Ministry of
Health, and similar agencies.

Responsibility for town planning in the Western Region is vested in the Town Planning Division of the Ministry
of Lands and Housing. This division is working on a regional
physical development plan, and it is hoped that this effort
will be coordinated with the investment policies of the regional development program through cooperation between the planning authorities and the Ministry of Economic Development.

Town planning authorities have been established in
twenty-two towns throughout the region. According to the
regional program, it was the intention of the government to
expand this number to 70, although there is little evidence
that this is to be done. More than Ł1.6 million were allocated by the Western Region in its program for 1962-68 to
expand and develop the town planning effort.

Of the twenty-two authorities, two are actively working on plans. One of these, the Ikeja Town Planning Authority in the northern portion of the Lagos metropolitan area
is directly responsible to the Ministry of Lands and Housing,
but cooperates with the Ikeja district council and sends an
observer to the meetings of the Lagos Executive Development
Board. It has a capable staff, which is preparing a physical
development plan for the town. Examination and approval of
construction permit applications, however, have engaged a
large part of the staff's time. Lack of funds has prevented it
from purchasing land to fulfill an expressed regional policy
of land acquisition.

As the town planning law of the Western Region does
not specify adequate means of financing for the town planning
authorities, they have depended upon permit fees and discretionary budget allocations from the ministry. The latter were
severely cut back after the political crisis in the region in
1962, as regional funds were extremely scarce and the political leaders did not set a high priority on town planning. The
entire budget of the Town Planning Division has been Ł25,000
per year in recent years. The senior staff of the Ikeja and

Ibadan Town Planning Authorities, as well as the central
staff, is paid out of this budget. These funds obviously could
not support twenty-two authorities, to say nothing of seventy.
The rest of the towns in the Western Region section of the
Lagos metropolitan area have no active zoning and town planning operations; physical development tends to be haphazard,
with little relationship between new construction and public
services.

PLANNING NEEDS

The National Development Plan, 1962-68, states,
"It is the government's intention that all development projects relating to the Lagos metropolitan area should be considered in the context of the over-all needs of the area. . . .
Unless an integrated programme is prepared for the Lagos
area as a whole, the present congestion and chaos would
undoubtedly worsen." There is little evidence that the political leadership has adopted this view or given it significant
weight.

None of the organizations engaged in planning activities that relate to Lagos is designed to take into consideration
the long-range development needs of the area as a whole or
to formulate coordinated priorities for investment and spatial
development. While the programs for Lagos scattered in the
National Development Plan do not appear to be incompatible,
neither are they explicitly complementary as to timing, location, development priorities, or ultimate impact on the shape
of the urban area. Together with the policy and organizational
problems, shortages of planning expertise, trained manpower, and reliable statistics contribute to this situation. *

---

* The data basis for planning in Lagos is extremely weak.
Outside the city limits there are scanty economic statistics,
and demographic data are unreliable. Within the federal
territory these are limited. The town planning section of
the Lagos Executive Development Board is currently undertaking social surveys in several sections of the city, but for
the most part the board relies on information gathered by
other agencies. The LEDB has inadequate research facilities. Financial and accounting data are rudimentary; data on

There is good evidence that these planning deficiencies are adversely affecting the impact of development investment in Lagos. Too narrow a range of factors is considered in the preparation of each project proposal. This is particularly evident in the slum-clearance scheme carried out on Lagos Island (which is described in Chapter 5). This project took little or no cognizance of the type of housing desired by the people it planned to rehouse, of the financial realities of the scheme, of its social implications, * or of the requirements for transportation and sewage facilities in the new settlement areas. Elsewhere, housing and industrial parks have been established without adequate supporting services. Because many of the designs for the City of Lagos do not look far enough ahead into the future, projects are often found inadequate after their completion, which necessitates extension or modification and consequently wastes resource.

Competition for land in federal territory is intense; prices are high, and there is little land on the market. Although the Ministry of Lagos Affairs and the Lagos Executive

----

consumption, incomes, distribution, and economic functions are scanty. The available statistics on education are far better than those in other areas, to the credit of the assistance of UNESCO personnel in establishing the program.

* Payment of an aggregate sum to families whose ancestral homes have been compulsorily acquired under the slum-clearance program has had a deleterious social effect. Although intended for use to purchase a substitute house elsewhere, it is usually seen as a windfall by those involved. The lump-sum payment to extended families raised competing claims from their members, and if divided among them left no one with adequate resources to build another house. The funds are dissipated by lawyers and individual claimants who quickly deplete their shares in unnecessary expenditure. The effect of this was a net decrease in number of houses, since alternative houses have not been built.
Wiser social policy might have been to provide a substitute freehold house to the entire family.

Development Board have been charged with coordinating the allocation of land in the city, this cannot be done in a rational way without land-use policies on which to base decisions and more rigid devices to resist specific pressures for land by politicians and persons of influence. Furthermore, because most new development is taking place to the north and the west of the city, metropolitan-wide alternatives of land development should be considered. In the meantime, there continues to be expensive reclamation of swamp land within the city as well as haphazard land development outside it, particularly along existing road routes to the north. The latter are already congested, for many job opportunities are centered in Lagos Island and Apapa in the south.

The United Nations team recommended planned development in the north of the metropolitan area on available land to the east and west of the present line of dense settlement in Bariga, Iwaya, and Shomolu (See Map 1). Its proposals included new commercial and residential clusters around existing village centers and a secondary central business district at Ikeja. The team also suggested developing Agege into a satellite city. Its rejection of stepped-up development to the west (beyond Ajegunle, where there is a great deal of available land) because new transportation services would be required is open to considerable argument. Residential and employment development could occur in that area with the result of shortening journeys to work. In any case, it is clear that only a comprehensive intergovernmental study and project planning effort could examine these alternatives thoroughly and rationalize development goals. The shape of the existing urban complex and low level of existing urban services underscore the importance of such an effort if investments in urban infrastructure are to improve urban life appreciably.

The recommendations of the United Nations team and those of Jones and Lucas for concentrating a comprehensive planning effort in a metropolitan development authority or a committee of a greater Lagos council were noted in Chapter 3. Other alternatives are available, of course. For example, the National Development Plan could incorporate an additional chapter that would embody a plan for the Lagos metropolitan area prepared jointly by Western Region and federal planning units and approved by both governments. Given the present system of public finance, under which most

capital projects are implemented by the federal or regional
government, it would be important to involve those governments in the planning stage. At the same time a general
spatial development policy for Lagos could be prepared by
a planning staff recruited, for example, from the Lagos
Executive Development Board or the Ministry of Housing
and from the Town Planning Division of the Western Region
government, if cooperative attitudes between the two governments should emerge. An all-inclusive master zoning
plan is not a necessary prerequisite to either of these approaches.

In any case, the effectiveness of any of the proposals
for comprehensive planning in Lagos are contingent upon new
patterns of communication and cooperation among the governments involved and considerable increase in financial and
manpower resources dedicated to planning. Moreover, each
operating agency must broaden its horizons in drawing up
project designs, both by taking into consideration the side
effects of its projects and by intensified accommodation to
the work of other agencies within the area.

Lagos is on the threshhold of major developments in
transit, housing, education, sewage, and water supply. Because the first giant steps are about to be taken in all of
these categories, there is a unique opportunity to harmonize
them in such a way as to influence the shape and directions
of metropolitan growth for many generations to come. This
is the strongest argument for the organization of a planning
effort that will consider the ramifications both in time and
space of major public investments.

PLAN IMPLEMENTATION

Most existing project plans for Lagos will be executed
by federal and regional ministries and corporations. The
minor exceptions are those projects of the Lagos City Council
that are sanctioned by the federal six-year program and account for less than 0. 5 per cent of the total commitment relating to Lagos in that program. Even these projects will
depend upon federal grants.

The statutory corporations and special authorities
play a very large role in plan implementation. They would

execute 42 per cent of the total public expenditure of the federal program. Of the Lagos projects, those for residential
building and industrial parks will be undertaken by the Lagos
Executive Development Board, the Nigerian Building Society,
the African Staff Housing Fund, the Western Nigeria Housing
Corporation, and the Western Nigeria Development Corporation. The Nigerian Railway Corporation and Nigerian Ports
Authority will carry out other improvements in Lagos. Many
observers have concluded that ministerial control over these
corporations should be intensified in order to ensure attainment of plan objectives. [2] Equally necessary are other state
control machineries to guard against corruption, which has
been prevalent in these corporations and which distort the
fulfillment of plan objectives and involve considerable loss
of public revenue. (Several inquiries are now being conducted into the affairs of Nigerian statutory corporations.)

There are few instances to date of direct conflict
between the view of a ministry or corporation responsible
for executing projects and the content of the plans, for the
latter have been based upon the operating agency's proposals.
The establishment of an interagency committee for Lagos,
however, as suggested in the National Development Plan,
might institute ongoing review and coordination of projects
implementation of comprehensive plans in the future. Experience in other urban areas has shown, however, that the
impact of such interministerial committees may be limited
unless superior political authority--such as that of the prime
minister--is utilized to achieve agreements and see that they
are carried out.

There have been progress reports prepared indicating
action taken in terms of the targets of the Nigerian National
Development Plan. The progress reports of 1963-64 indicate
that it is inaction rather than action contrary to plan policies
that is the major stumbling block to plan implementation.
Several federal and regional agencies simply reported "no
progress."

At the federal and regional levels there are some
other special procedures designed to enhance plan implementation. A federal minister must apply to the Ministry of Finance for authorization of credit to undertake plan projects.
Two committees pass on these project proposals: the Permanent Committee of Officials and the Ministerial Economic

Committee.   The first includes staff from several ministries
and departments, while the second consists of ministers
themselves.   The ministerial committee has the power to
authorize the projects and specify the sources of capital finance.   Both of the committees rely on the policies of the
National Development Plan and on the order of priorities
prepared by the Joint Planning Committee.

The Ministerial Economic Committee has also prepared an annual capital budget consistent with the plan.   The
Economic Planning Unit advises the ministries and corporations in drawing up their budget proposals.

The planning officials feel that the main responsibility
for coordinated implementation of the plan should lie with the
planning authority itself; a proposal that the National Economic Committee form a subcommittee of representatives of
the federal government and the regions endowed with coordinating powers over plan execution is under consideration.

In the regions, plan execution has been the responsibility of the executive councils, which have established working committees to attempt to ensure coordination in the application of the plan.

The budget process of the Lagos City Council is not
directly related to any plans.   The annual city budget includes a capital budget divided into two sections: (1) capital
projects to be financed by loans and grants; and (2) capital
projects to be financed from current earnings.   These budgets do not extend beyond three years.   They are prepared
in the same way as the general operating budget and consist
of the immediate capital requirements of the city departments.

The repeated problems of project execution experienced within Lagos have been inadequate commitment of
funds--sometimes traceable to unrealistic cost estimates--
and complaints by the technical officers in the operating
agencies that the Ministry of Lagos Affairs interfered too
frequently and without adequate information.   Shortage of
funds has been aggravated by financial waste resulting from
the corruption of officers of the city government, in league
with councilors, and the limited competence of contractors.
The major obstacles to plan implementation at this stage,

aside from the weaknesses of the plans themselves, are the
fundamental administrative deficiencies in Lagos--particu-
larly shortage of trained manpower--and widespread and recurrent incidence of irregularity.

Finally, if a comprehensive spatial plan is developed
for Lagos, control of land use and construction would be an
important, if negative, mode of applying it. At present, the
Lagos Executive Development Board is responsible for exercising land-use controls within the federal territory, such
as zoning, issuance of building permits, and allocation of
sites for public purposes. The LEDB has classified land
for residential, industrial, commercial, and social uses
and for varying degrees of density. Sites for recreation,
education, and cemeteries have been zoned. All construction
in the city is contingent upon review of building plans by the
LEDB, which applies zoning regulations and building standards relating to obstructions; plot sizes; open space between
buildings; balconies; sizes of kitchens, bathrooms and la-
trines; sanitary facilities; ventilation; height of building;
provision for sidewalks and parking space. If the LEDB
approves the application, it is forwarded to the Lagos City
Council, which issues the permit.

The building and zoning regulations do not require
extension of public services or minimum service standards.
For the most part, throughout the metropolitan area new
settlement has far preceded extension of public services
except in the cases of estates planned and constructed by
the Lagos Executive Development Board or the Western Nigerian Housing Corporation, for which electricity, water
supply, roads, and septic tanks have been arranged.

Further controls may prove necessary to attain any
patterns chosen by a comprehensive plan. These will be
difficult to enforce, however, for land rights and ownership
are firmly entrenched in Nigerian tradition, and land is a
common form of savings. Above all, a long history of unregistered customary land transfers and extended-family
tenure complicates administration of controls. On the other
hand, as the role of the private sector in large-scale development of land in Lagos is minor, the influence of public
projects on future development patterns can be great.

NOTES TO CHAPTER 4

1.   Federal Government of Nigeria, National Development Plan of Nigeria, 1962-68 (Lagos: Government Printers, 1962), p. 22.

2.   See, for example: United Nations Meeting of Experts on Administrative Aspects of National Development Planning, The Administration of Planning in Nigeria (Paris: 1964). Mimeo.

CHAPTER 5 SELECTED URBAN
SERVICES IN LAGOS

All of the public services examined in this chapter--
water supply, passenger transportation, public housing, and
education--are in extremely short supply in the Lagos metropolitan area. Large-scale capital expansion has been proposed for all four in the National Development Plan and by
the United Nations team that surveyed the needs of the metropolis in 1963. While the agencies involved in these service
categories vary--from city department to federal ministry,
including public corporations operating at local, regional,
and federal levels--all the major improvements proposed
would require federal financing.

WATER SUPPLY

A single agency, Lagos Water Supply, undertakes to
supply, treat, and distribute public water in the metropolitan area. Lagos Water Supply is a subdivision of the federal
Ministry of Works and Housing.* By statute, it is authorized
to operate within the Federal Territory of Lagos, but it in
fact serves several towns outside the city limits. This expansion of jurisdiction occurred informally in response to
population growth in Shomolu, Mushin, Ikeja, Maryland
Estate, and some other towns in the urban area, where
growing demands for water were not met by other governmental authorities. Extension of its supply area will probably continue in this way.

---

* Prior to 1966, this was the Ministry of Works and Survey. Housing was the responsibility of the Ministry of Lagos
Affairs and, in 1965, of a new Ministry of Housing, which
was merged with the Ministry of Works in 1966.

The organization is a line agency headed by a chief engineer who reports to the director of works of the ministry. The director of works, in turn, consults with the permanent secretary but accounts directly to the minister for most purposes.

The agency is divided into two operating sections--production and distribution--in addition to accounting and executive offices. The production section, located at the Iju Waterworks, north of the metropolitan area (see Map 1), is responsible for water abstraction, purification, and storage. It is managed by a senior water engineer. Under his management are several officers with distinct responsibilities: the water engineer, headworks; chemist; mechanical engineer; and chief waterworks superintendent. The remainder of the staff includes chemical laboratory assistants, superintendents, electricians, boiler men, clerks, and other employees.

The distribution section is headquartered in Ijora, in the city, and is managed by the senior water engineer for distribution, under whom are several sectional heads: the water engineer for distribution, the water engineer for records, chief water superintendents, and other junior staff (see Chart 2).

The senior officers of Lagos Water Supply are selected by the Nigerian Public Service Commission on the basis of established qualifications and in accordance with statutory procedures. The director of works of the ministry can make recommendations concerning tenure, promotion, and disciplinary matters, but these too are subject to the authority of the commission. Personnel of lesser rank are handled by the director of works or are left to the chief engineer of Lagos Water Supply.

The water supply agency undertakes all the operations necessary to provide public water in the area, from construction and operation of pumps, treatment plants, and storage tanks to distribution and metering. It constructs mains and pipes for supply to private and commercial establishments free of charge, except when a company or tenant requests immediate service that the agency cannot provide. In such a case, it may authorize the consumer to construct pipe lines and mains at his own expense. In the Western

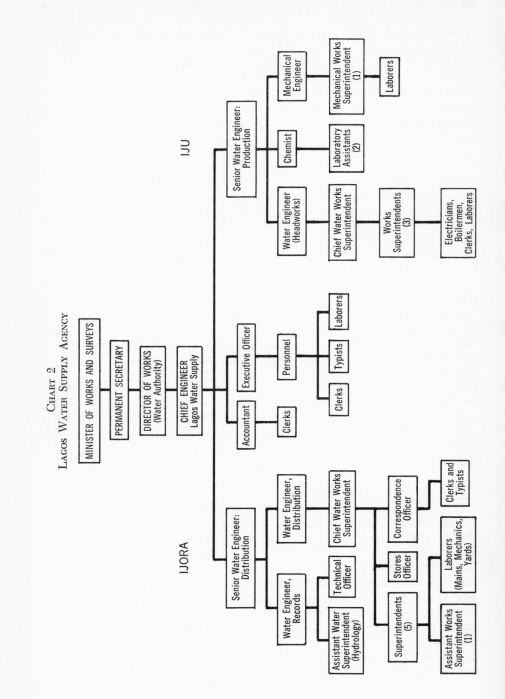

CHART 2
LAGOS WATER SUPPLY AGENCY

Region section of the service area, the regional government is responsible for meter installation but Lagos Water Supply undertakes repair, reading, and replacement of existing meters. The water supply agency is legally empowered to construct public taps and fountains; to inspect any facility for waste or damage; to connect or disconnect pipes to any dwelling; and to demand fees for excess consumption and meter rent from tenants.

The Lagos City Council, through the water and sewage section of the city engineer's department, plays a subsidiary role in water supply within the city limits. It contributes annually to operating finance by paying an aggregate sum, agreed upon in advance, to the water supply agency. It collects water taxes within the city, which partially compensate for this outlay.

Lagos Water Supply provides purified water to domestic consumption points, and directly to industrial users whose water consumption is metered. Domestic consumption is not metered and is subsidized by the city council. The local water tax is levied by the city council on the value of residential buildings at a rate of 6 pence (d.) per pound (Ł) of assessed valuation. In 1962-63, the council realized Ł15, 644 from collection of the water taxes and paid Ł40, 000 to Lagos Water Supply. The federal government further subsidizes domestic consumption through the budget of the water supply agency, for the price it receives from the city is below costs of production and distribution. Thus the Lagos City Council neither buys nor sells water at an economic rate. *

----

* The Lagos City Council purchases bulk water from Lagos Water Supply at a price that has amounted to approximately 2s. 6d. per 1, 000 gallons. Costs to Lagos Water Supply, however, are in the region of 3s. per 1, 000 gallons. Thus, the federal government is absorbing slightly more than 6d. per 1, 000 gallons consumed in city homes. The magnitude of the federal subsidy tends to become greater than these figures indicate, however. As consumption rises, the city council gains, since it pays an agreed sum which is fixed and does not reflect any increase in consumption or in capital outlay by Lagos Water Supply.

The payment made by the city council to Lagos Water
Supply represents less than a quarter of the agency's actual
expenditure, which was Ł170,000 in 1962-63. Roughly 60
per cent of the total revenues of the agency are derived from
the sale of water to the Lagos City Council and to all other
consumers, whom it charges directly (i.e., all consumers
outside the city and industrial and commercial consumers
inside the city). The remainder is derived from the general
federal budget. *

The rates directly charged to consumers by Lagos
Water Supply vary from 8s. 6d. per 1,000 gallons to vessels
at the wharfs, to 6d. per 1,000 gallons to swimming and
sports clubs. Domestic water use outside the city is free of
charge up to a certain consumption level, after which the

---

* The National Development Plan estimates that operating
revenue of Lagos Water Supply was Ł491,000 short of current costs (wages, other administrative costs, depreciation,
and 6 per cent on capital) in 1961-62; would be Ł812,000
short in 1965-66; and Ł1,010,000 short in 1967-68, given
planned expansion and present charges. On the other hand,
the plan estimates that if the price structure were evened out
and metering extended so that 80 per cent of all water distributed was sold at the rate of 2s. 6d. per 1,000 gallons, costs
would be covered by 1964-65, and a 5.8 per cent rate of return could be reached by 1968. Present cost figures given
by the water supply agency indicate these estimates are op-
timistic. In any case, they assume extension of metering to
private, industrial, and commercial users and increased
charges to the Lagos City Council.
Unfortunately, complete metering is not feasible in the
short run from the technical, administrative, and financial
standpoints. Weather conditions and the low level of the
water table quickly impair meters and render them inoper-
able in Lagos. Further, the cost of meters is high relative
to individual household consumption, and grouping of several
households for metering purposes would prove a source of
constant friction. The water tax seems a workable alternative since there is some rough correlation between building
valuation and the volume of water consumption per household
or group of households. With this approach, wastage is a
persistent problem, but the cost of effective inspection and

excess consumption is charged at the rate of 2s. 6d. per
1, 000 gallons. At nine public selling stations in Ikeja and
Agege, * water is sold at one-tenth penny per 4 gallons
(which is equal to about 2s. 1d. per 1, 000 gallons).

The dual structure of water charges results in the
consumer in the Western Region portion of the metropolitan
area paying far higher prices for water than the taxpayer in
the city.

Appraisal of Water Supply

Although there are no figures as to the population
directly reached by the public water supply system in
metropolitan Lagos, it is estimated that some 600, 000 people
(more than 90 per cent of its population) are served within
the city. In addition, at least 50 per cent of the population
of the Western Region sections of the urban area is served.

The distribution system, however, consists of three
types of outlets: (1) water borne directly to commercial
establishments and single-family dwellings; (2) water borne
to dwelling outlets serving several families (nuclear or
extended families in compounds); and (3) water borne to
neighborhood taps. Of the total population in the Lagos
metropolitan area, roughly 10 per cent are served by the
first, 55 per cent by the second, and 20 per cent by the
third type of outlet. The remaining inhabitants utilize
streams or private wells or buy water from their neighbors.
It is not uncommon for families with taps in their dwelling
units to sell water to their neighbors at a 1, 500 per cent
profit.

----

other measures to reduce waste are comparatively cheaper
than metering. Moreover, any widespread metering effort
at this time would require establishment of a meter industry
or considerable foreign exchange for meter imports.

* Of these, two at Agege and one at Ikeja are run by the federal government and an additional six at Ikeja are run by an
officer of the regional government. The revenues are paid
to Lagos Water Supply.

The patterns of distribution and systems of water charges result in severe inequities among various sectors of the population both as to the availability of potable water and as to its costs.   Throughout the area there is intensive distribution to public and commercial buildings and to high-income residential areas.   Low-income, dense settlements are served by sparse standpipes, while some sections are not served at all.

The public water supply for Lagos is drawn from Iju and Ogun rivers.   The water passes through pumping and treatment plants to a service reservoir at Shaga that has a capacity of 6.7 million gallons.   From the service reservoir, there are three feeder mains--of 42 inches, 28 inches, and 24 inches in diameter, respectively--which feed into the network of distribution mains varying in diameter from 3 to 6 inches.   Consumers are supplied through connecting pipes and public fountains and standpipes (of which there are 375) in the city itself.   Due to the topography of Lagos, there are no suitable sites for large reservoirs within 15 miles of the supply area; daily fluctuations in demand are handled by twelve elevated storage tanks.   Industrial consumers and high-income domestic users frequently provide their own facilities for storage of a one-day supply of water.

While the water distributed is consistently safe by health standards, dysentery and diarrhea are the third highest cause of death in Lagos, and the medical officer of the city council estimates that over 80 per cent of school children are infested with intestinal parasites.   The infant mortality rate is extremely high--62.9 per 1,000 live births in 1960. The major contributing conditions to these health problems, however, are the lack of water-borne sewage and the overcrowded living conditions.   The quality of the existing water supply system, which was introduced in 1914, is largely responsible for the fact that there have not been epidemic expansions of disease.

The quantity of potable water must be rapidly increased, however, not only to parallel population growth but also to expand service to populations relying on wells and streams (as in Isolo, Iwaya, and Ajegunle) and to provide water for a sewage system, if health hazards are not to increase.   Population growth has placed severe strains on the system's capacity although it has continually been expanded

since 1958. Increasingly severe low-pressure periods
during the annual dry season could cause infiltration of
ground water, which is heavily polluted with sewage. It is
occasionally necessary during the dry season to stop supply
for some hours a day.

There have been no thorough geological analyses, but
it is believed that ground water sources have little potential,
for, apart from sewage saturation, most of Lagos lies below
sea level. A small river to the west of Lagos, the Iwo River,
could be exploited in the future; but a more lasting solution
seems to lie in tapping the Ogun River upstream some 60
miles into the Western Region.

The consumption of water remains very close to the
capacity of the system. The total amount of purified water
supplied in the area in 1964 was about 6.5 billion gallons,
averaging 18 million gallons per day. Average daily consumption in February, 1965, was 15.9 million gallons in the
city and 2.39 million gallons in the rest of the service area.
(These figures demonstrate the severe deficiencies in the
Western Region, where nearly half the metropolitan population is located.) Total demand in August, 1966, was 21.8
million gallons per day.

Planned Capital Improvements

Between 1958 and 1965 the capacity of the water supply system for Lagos was increased by 165 per cent from 9
million gallons per day to 24 million gallons. This expansion
took place in two stages. First, between 1958 and 1959,
major extensions of the headworks, trunk mains, and distribution systems were undertaken, including a new pumping
station on the Iju River and additional pumps and purification
facilities at the Ogun intake. These improvements brought
capacity to about 16 million gallons per day. Between 1962
and 1965, three projects were started to implement the targets of the National Development Plan (1962-68). The goals
for Lagos water supply set forth in the federal program of
the plan are to reach an average capacity of 40 million gallons per day by 1968 and extend the service area from 34 to
70 square miles.

These targets were designed to accommodate metropolitan growth to over 1 million people as well as industrial

expansion. Per capita consumption would remain low--about
24 gallons per person per day. The investment allocation of
the plan to carry out water supply extension is Ł1. 8 million.

The three projects underway are: (1) hydrological
survey of the Ogun River preparatory to future extensions;
(2) the "Water Supply Lagos" project, which involves additional facilities at the Ogun station and new mains leading
from it to Iju, and from Iju to the storage reservoir; and
(3) the "Development of Lagos Water Supply" project, under
which the capacity of the Iju system has been increased from
16 to 18. 5 million gallons per day by construction of a new
pump and mains.

The whole burden of implementing the water expansion plan rests with Lagos Water Supply, which undertakes
both project design and execution. These projects will continue for some years and the total capital expenditure on
them is now estimated at slightly over Ł2 million. Only
Ł167, 000 was expended, however, from 1962 to 1964. The
work is financed by the federal government in the capital
budget of the works division of the Ministry of Works. A
final draft of this budget is reviewed by the director of works
(who is the formal "water authority") and the permanent
secretary of the ministry. Informal approval of the minister
is given, after which the estimates go to the Ministry of
Finance and the National Economic Committee for approval
before being submitted to Parliament for appropriation.

It is clear from rates of capital expenditure and work
between 1962 and 1965 that the targets will not be met by 1968.
This is in large part due to parliamentary reluctance to meet
adequate capital costs above and beyond operating water subsidies.

A far more ambitious plan for expansion of Lagos
water supply has been submitted to the federal government
by the United States Agency for International Development.
This plan is designed to expand the system to a capacity of
84 million gallons per day (over three times 1965 capacity)
to meet the demands of a population predicted at 2 million
by 1975, while increasing per capita daily consumption to at
least 40 gallons. It would be implemented jointly by the
Ministry of Works and the USAID. Capital expenditure of

Ƚ17. 9 million would be made over a period of ten years, financed by a USAID long-term, low-interest loan.

Although the full details of the plan are not known, there is no evidence that the forecasts or the design of the plan proposals were correlated to concepts of land use and other aspects of development of the metropolitan area. The demand for water projected for 1975 does not seem to take account of construction of a central sewage system, which is under consideration by the federal government.

Several administrative steps are necessary to give effect to this plan. The technical officers of the Ministry of Works must advise the division director of that ministry that the plan is feasible and sound. (A feasibility study has been conducted.) The director of works, after discussing the matter with the permanent secretary of the ministry, will then be referred to the cabinet for approval and subsequently to the Ministry of Finance, which must examine and approve the loan agreement. From this stage on, implementation on the Nigerian side will be by the Ministry of Works and Ministry of Finance.

The USAID plan includes a proposal to modify the organization of water supply administration, which has given rise to some controversy. USAID recommended that a corporation-type structure, operating on economic grounds and with jurisdiction over the entire urban area, should take over the water supply function. This water authority or board would be independent of the civil service and the operating procedures of the ministry in its day-to-day planning and operations. The proposal has met with understandable opposition in the works division of the ministry. The ministry favors continued inclusion of the water agency within its structure.

Factors of financial management underlie proposals for reorganization of water supply in Lagos. * The existing

------

* A semi-independent metropolitan water board was first proposed by a federal study group in 1960. Later, Jones and Lucas recommended turning water supply over to an elected greater Lagos council, while the UN assistance team

agency responded to felt demands outside the city limits as
the urban area expanded, but the de facto extension of its
service area has not been incorporated into law; the Western
Region remains formally responsible for water supply in its
portion of the Lagos urban area.   Three problems have
emerged.   First, there are considerable differences in services received and rates paid by different sections of the
population.   Second, the pricing system does not produce
revenues to meet operating costs and, therefore, puts more
burden on the public budgets than may be necessary. *   Third,
capital resources allocated to Lagos Water Supply have been
insufficient to achieve planned rates of expansion.   There is
intense competition for scarce federal capital from manifold
other high-priority investment programs.   Water supply,
which is not a legal responsibility of the federal government
outside the city limits, is not in a strong position to compete.   All of these problems could be mitigated by financial
changes and intergovernmental agreements between federal
and regional authorities without abolishing the present water
supply agency, which has a relatively good performance
record.   The offer of foreign assistance from USAID, which
has been made contingent upon structural and financial reorganization, may force the issue.

     In contrast with the USAID emphasis on economically
sound operation conducive to capital improvement, the Ministry of Works insists that water supply is primarily a social

----

proposed to assign it to the metropolitan development agency.
The Western Region government has removed water supply
from local authority responsibility and established a regional
water board (which does not plan to service any part of the
Lagos metropolitan area).   The existing trend of ad hoc expansion of the Lagos Water Supply Agency's service area,
however, has followed the path of least resistance by avoiding
the boundary problem, which reorganization proposals stumble
over.

* The United Nations team recommended that water prices
should cover both operating costs, and amortization and interest for capital investment.   The National Development
Plan proposes that water prices be raised to meet operating
costs and provide a growing rate of return on capital.

service that requires subsidy. The social service aspects of water supply in Lagos cannot be dismissed. Because per capital water consumption is low, any upgrading of the water prices that would restrict water use on the part of the poor would have negative effects on public health conditions. This exception to the principle of self-financing should be taken into consideration in any effort to revise the price structure (for example, the present practice of providing a minimum quantity of water per family free before application of charges might be maintained). Changes in the price structure could be designed, however, to shift some of the present burden from low-income groups by complete metering of industry, ships, and public buildings and by raising tax rates within the city. And increased water charges could increase the capacity to extend the system to people who are not now served, thereby extending the benefits from a social service point of view.

Most of the commentators agree that the functions of supply and water pricing within the city should be vested in the same authority. The Lagos City Council, which sets the water tax rates within the city, has an immediate political interest in maintaining a subsidy to city users. While there has been little public opinion expressed in relation to water supply in recent years, public rallies and protest meetings in the city have held down water rates in the past. In recent years, the press seems to be the only channel through which occasional comments on the administration or planning of the water system are aired, as during shortages in 1964 and 1965. Proposals to raise rates appreciably in the city, however, may generate new protests, which it may be very difficult for the city council to resist. A middle-ground alternative would be to turn over metering and rating powers within the city to Lagos Water Supply, but to vest local government with powers of approval over rates, with the stipulation that if it refuses to approve rates that cover operating costs, it must provide compensating subsidies to the water supply agency. This arrangement is utilized in several other areas of the world.

On the whole, the present system is relatively well managed. Preliminary investigations by the water supply agency have indicated that there is a wastage of about 10 to 20 per cent of the total quantity of water delivered in the supply systems. At present, the agency is actively engaged

in an effort to reduce such wastage through inspection and
public education. Its operations suffer mainly from shortages in technical staff, particularly in the light of the demands upon it generated by expansion. There is only one
engineer in charge of distribution, inadequate manpower to
manage a system of this size. In the opinion of the officials
of Lagos Water Supply, the supply area should be divided into
about nine zones, each with a superintendent, but there are
only four or five superintendents within the staff. Operating
personnel must undertake survey and planning work, and the
chemical and laboratory staff is far below what is needed.
As the system embarks on large-scale expansion, a fully
staffed planning and survey office should be instituted. This
staffing pattern seems to be the key problem of water supply
administration that is skirted by the public corporation proposal.

The need for a continuing water planning effort is
manifest in the fact that existing projections for future water
needs will prove inadequate if a central sewage system is
constructed in Lagos, if growth of the population continues
at present rates, if extension of the supply area is carried
out, and if desired rises in the standards of living and personal hygiene take place. There has been no reconciliation
between USAID projections of demands for water and those
proposed by national plan and the water supply agency.

Sewage

Because the lack of sewage systems in Lagos is its
most severe urban problem and is so closely related to future
needs for water supply, it deserves comment here. At
present, the city water and sewage section in the engineer's
department operates disposal services consisting of: a few
underground sewers serving some institutions and city wards
that discharge sewage into the lagoon; cleaning of septic
tanks in favored areas of the city such as Apapa, Ikoyi, and
recently built low- and medium-density residential areas;
and collection of some 18,000 pails of night soil, which are
loaded onto tractor-driven tanks and emptied in the lagoon.
These services are handled partially through city contracts
with private operators.

In the Western Region portion of the metropolitan
area, residents must arrange and pay for disposal privately.

Federal proposals in 1959-62 to extend the boundaries of the
federal territory were partially justified in terms of requirement for a metropolitan-wide sewage system.

The active issue at present, however, concerns the
creation of a comprehensive underground sewage system for
the city. This has been proposed at various times since
1902. In 1956, the project was revived and preliminary construction of sewage tanks was begun, but the problem of financing the project, which was then estimated to cost Ŀ8. 5-
Ŀ9 million, was not resolved. The Lagos City Council supported the project but the federal government rejected it as
too expensive. During the preparation of the present National Development Plan, it was agreed that this was an urgent and important work, but most experts have concluded
that it requires foreign aid.

In addition to the financial problems, there are several technical problems involved, the first being that in parts
of Lagos the water table is near the surface. Second, there
are some existing septic tanks and pumps in Lagos but the
federal government has not yet approved a city council re-
quest for funds to connect them by pipes. The federal Ministry of Works does not support transformation of the Lagos
disposal system into a complex network of septic tanks and
pipelines. Thus, piecemeal investments previously made
are bringing little or no return of benefits.

The third difficulty, which is linked with the problem
of finance, concerns the dysfunction between the sewage
needs of various localities in the urban area and their financial resources--as between the commercial centers, where
heavy taxes can be levied for construction of a septic tank
system, and the dense residential areas, where construction
of such a system would be expensive but is most needed.

There are now several proposals for a central Lagos
sewage system under consideration. Both a United Nations
technical-assistance team and a private company have undertaken studies of the problem, but their project proposals
have not been released by the government. In addition, the
Lagos City Council recently sent a study team to the Soviet
Union to discuss the Moscow sewage system and possibilities
of foreign aid. According to available information the Soviets

are willing to make a loan toward construction of a sewage system and to send technicians to supervise the project.

Finally, however, the proceedings of the Saville Commission of Inquiry into the Lagos City Council have brought to light an "antisewage" clique in the council, which has a private financial interest in existing public contracts for the conservancy services.

MASS PASSENGER TRANSPORTATION

A major feature of the mass movement of people in the Lagos metropolitan area is the dominance of three destinations near the extremities of the urban complex: Lagos Island, Apapa, and Ikeja. It is to and from these points of job concentration that the linear transportation routes lie. Within this pattern, the focal point of transportation and congestion is the Carter Bridge, which spans the series of islands that form the older part of Lagos and part of the mainland where the newer urban area lies. It is the only point of contact by road between Lagos Island and Apapa, and between Lagos Island and the Western Region.

Existing transportation services in Lagos are of four types. The Lagos City Transport Service (LCTS) operates buses throughout the urban area. The Nigerian Railway Corporation runs commuter trains between Agege, Ikeja, Oshodi, and Apapa. The Inland Waterway Board, a subdivision of the Ministry of Transport and Aviation, operates ferry service between Lagos Island and Apapa. And finally, there are diverse private passenger vehicles—from buses to dilapidated trucks and taxis.

Altogether, about 120, 000 people traveled into Lagos Island each weekday in 1965 and about as many traveled out. This number is increasing by roughly 4 per cent per year. The United Nations team estimated in 1962 that the traffic in both directions over the Carter Bridge was composed as follows: 30, 000 pedestrians; 50, 000 bicyclists; 100, 000 LCTS bus passengers; 30, 000 private bus passengers; and 30, 000 private automobiles. Other passengers use ferries and private boats. While automobile usage is relatively low, it is very rapidly increasing. In 1961, there were 14, 000 licensed motor vehicles in the city itself (excluding

motorcycles, of which there were 3,000). The number of
cars crossing the Carter Bridge is mounting by about 12 per
cent per year. In addition, the commuter trains carry about
9,000 passengers in both directions within the urban area per
day.

Lagos City Transport Service

Public transport is dominated by the Lagos City
Transport Service (LCTS) buses. LCTS buses operate
throughout the federal territory, and, since 1961, their
routes have been extended to Ikeja in the Western Region.
The major part of the service is concentrated, however,
in the city; in 1964, the Yaba to Lagos Island route alone
accounted for 20 of the 100 buses then operated by the
LCTS, and 5 other intracity routes accounted for an additional 42 buses. The service operated a total of 102 buses
in February, 1965,* and 136 buses in July, 1966.

The Lagos City Transport Service does not have
autonomous legal existence, but is formally a department
of the Lagos City Council operated under the direction of
the Lagos City Transport Board. This board was established
in March, 1964, by federal statute (City Transport Regulations Act of 1964), by which it was given responsibility to
determine the policies governing transport services and to
provide and administer such services within the City of Lagos and adjoining areas. Prior to this time, control of the
service was vested exclusively in the city council.

The transport board includes six members appointed
by the minister of Lagos affairs. Of these, five are from the
Lagos City Council, and one, a businessman of considerable
experience, was chosen from the general public. In addition,
there are three ex officio members: the city clerk, the city
treasurer, and the general manager of the Lagos City Transport Service. A chairman, appointed by the minister of Lagos affairs, presides over its meetings, which by law must
convene at least once a month.

---

* On a sample day in February, 1965, the total number of
passengers carried by the LCTS buses was 144,334.

The transport service itself is headed by a general manager, who is appointed by and is accountable to the Transport Board. He is responsible for day-to-day control and administration of the transport services, and the board may delegate to him any powers it wishes.

The service remains, however, legally a city council department, although a special layer of control--the transport board--has been inserted between the council itself and the operation of the service. While this board represents the council (and takes the place of a council committee) and the city bureaucracy, it is appointed and controlled by the minister and has independent statutory powers.

Local civil service regulations apply to officials of the LCTS. No high-ranking officer may be appointed without approval of the minister of Lagos affairs (henceforth of the minister of Internal affairs). * Personnel administration is otherwise entrusted to the general manager of the service, for the transport board has delegated to him the power to supervise and control the acts of all city officers involved in transport services, and to set conditions of work, pay, privileges, and allowances. Discipline of the officers of the LCTS is conditioned by their level as well as by the procedure of their appointment. Responsibility for the discipline of a junior employee rests with his sectional head and the personnel officer, both of whom must agree on a disciplinary measure before it is referred to the general manager for approval. However, disciplinary measure against an employee whose appointment was approved by the board is subject to the review of the board, while that of an employee approved by the minister is subject to review by him. A disciplined employee may, however, appeal to an independent tribunal as provided for in the City Transport Regulations Act. The general manager usually exercises his powers in consultation with the chairman of the board and the minister when high-ranking officers are involved. The administrative secretary of the LCTS, the accountant, the works manager, and

---

* Appointment of junior employees with salaries under Ł400 per annum is by the personnel officer in conjunction with the head of the section where the vacancy occurs; appointment to posts with salaries of Ł400 and over must be by advertisement and interview with approval of the board in some cases; appointment to post with a salary of Ł900 or more must be with the approval of the ministry.

traffic manager are the four department heads reporting immediately to the general manager of the service.

The LCTS is financed by its earnings and is subsidized neither by the federal government nor by the city council. Its profits accrue to the council and are utilized for other municipal activities. The transport service submits an annual financial report to the city council, * and through it, to the minister. By use of approval powers over both capital and operating expenditure, however, the ministry can issue and enforce directives to the service management.

Proposals for capital expenditure by the LCTS must be submitted by the general manager to the transport board. If the service's capital reserve can cover the expenditure, recommendation is forwarded to the Lagos City Council for approval and, ultimately, to the minister for authorization. If the service's capital reserve cannot cover the expenditure, the Lagos City Council must provide (with approval of the minister) an interest-free loan to the service, which is repaid as profits are realized.

Operating expenditure by the LCTS has been growing rapidly in recent years. ** The gross revenues of the service (which are derived entirely from its own income and of which 90 per cent is from transportation fares) are also rising. Passengers carried rose from 37. 4 million in 1961-62 to 50. 1 million in 1965-66. Profits turned over to the Lagos City Council, however, diminished from 1959 through

---

* The accounts of the LCTS are subject to external audit periodically by the Federal Government Audit Department. Further control of LCTS expenditure depends on internal audit, and the restriction of the power to sign checks for it to the city treasurer or his deputy.

** Its expenditure has been as follows: 1962-63: Ŀ728, 100; 1963-64: Ŀ872, 247; 1964-65: Ŀ940, 600. The budget is broken down into three categories, which were for 1964-65 as follows: Workshop Operating Accounts: Ŀ214, 250; Omnibus Operating Account: Ŀ498, 950; Administration and Establishment Expenses: Ŀ89, 710.

1963, showing a rise in 1964 associated with extension of routes and concomitant increase in passenger volume.*

While increased costs reflect wage rises, profits of the service have been adversely affected in addition by operating inefficiency, corruption, and pilferage. Both public attitudes and an inadequate supervisory staff have contributed to these conditions.

In the LCTS accounts for 1960-62, the city treasurer wrote:

> ... lower standard of efficiency has manifested itself in different ways. It is common knowledge that many Lagos City Transport Service drivers are bad drivers. This has resulted in a very high accident rate resulting in considerable damage to vehicles, not to talk of third party liability arising from such accidents, and the average amount spent on maintenance of every bus per annum is about Ⱡ750. This is a very high figure. It certainly does not justify the large number of breakdowns recorded. If breakdowns are to be reduced to a minimum, workshop efficiency accompanied by suitable disciplinary measures must be increased.

Apart from the question of competency, the public feels that there is an obvious lack of courtesy on the part of bus conductors. Moreover, there are two or three conductors to a bus where one could do the job.

Finally, the problem of pilferage plagues the revenue collections of the LCTS. Inspectors are not always on duty to check the buses--or when on duty, they do little checking-- with the result that the conductors are able to defraud the service. Riders frequently pay half fare in return for not

---

* Profits dropped from Ⱡ158,000 in 1959-60 to Ⱡ112,000 in 1962-63; rose to Ⱡ187,000 in 1963-64 and dropped to Ⱡ185,000 in 1964-65. Fares range from 3 to 10 pence, depending on mileage zones.

receiving tickets, with the understanding that the amount paid is pocketed by the conductor. In addition, a great number of government staff travel alone or with friends and with families free of charge, although not so authorized.

In summary, deficiencies in financial control, technical expertise, staff training, and supervision account for a good deal of the service's problems. The city treasurer has made recommendations for improvement that have not been implemented. The city council has been reluctant to take firm steps over the management of the transit service, which has operated with de facto autonomy. The transit board was instituted with the ostensible purpose of intensifying control over the service and mitigating the impact on it of council politics. It appears, however, that the board device did not alter prevailing patterns of behavior. Illegal practices have, in fact, involved board members. The proceedings before the Saville Commission of Inquiry in 1966 revealed rolling stock costs that are inflated by kickbacks to the decision makers and to some extent purchase of unsuitable equipment.

Other Services

Four private bus companies operate about 100 buses, which serve Lagos Island, Suru-Lere, Shomolu, Idi-Oro, Yaba, Apapa, and other points on the mainland. The private companies operate under permits granted by the Lagos City Council to supplement the services of the LCTS. A condition of their licensing was an agreement that new buses would not be added to their existing rolling stock so that the private operators would be eliminated by attrition. (As demands for bus services far exceed what the LCTS can provide, a sensible alternative would be for the local authorities to enter into agreements with the private companies for continued services with revenues shared with the government, until such time as public authorities are able to provide sufficient transit services.)

In addition, there are some 750 to 800 "mammywagons" (all manner of trucks used for passenger travel), minibuses, and other transport vehicles licensed to operate in the federal territory and still others licensed by the Western Region.

While the private transportation proprietors are subject to traffic, safety, and fare regulations by the Lagos City
Council, enforcement is weak. The trucks are scheduled
poorly or not at all and are extremely uncomfortable and
sometimes unsafe. They are concentrated along one or two
major roads that traverse the urban area, thus adding to
congestion. Restrictions on the number of passengers and
the quality of vehicles are seldom, if ever, enforced, and
the trucks stop and park in traffic lanes, creating bottle-
necks. The Lagos City Council has prohibited taxis and
trucks licensed in the Western Region from operating in
the federal territory, but this ban has proved almost impossible to enforce. The most recent attempt to enforce
the city bylaws resulted in a "park-in" organized by the
motor transport drivers and owners unions that brought
traffic in Lagos to a standstill in May, 1965, and succeeded
in forcing the city to cease enforcement efforts.

There are no subsidies given to the private transport
firms in general, and no contractual agreements have been
entered into between them and the government authorities.
In any case, the operation by private firms in transportation
has been by small entrepreneurs with little or no capital
resources.

The railroad line serving the Lagos urban area is
managed by the Nigerian Railway Corporation, which has
exclusive responsibility for railroad transportation throughout Nigeria. Apapa is the terminus of a major line to the
interior of Nigeria. Commuter trains on this line run from
Apapa to Agege, with several stops in between. The railway
corporation is the largest public corporation in the nation.
Constituted by the federal government, its directing board is
appointed by the minister of transport and aviation, to whom
its chairman is responsible. The railroad, which has no
separate accounts or departments concerned with Lagos commuter service, has operated at a deficit. The current
National Development Plan proposes that modernization investments should be made to put the railroad on an economic
basis.

Finally, the Inland Waterways Board, which is a subdivision of the federal Ministry of Transport and Aviation,
operates a ferry service between Lagos Island and Apapa
that carries a total of approximately 15,000 passengers

daily. This is a line agency of the ministry subject to the coordinating management of the permanent secretary and the policy direction of the minister.

Because public passenger transportation in Lagos is dominated by bus services, its efficiency is highly contingent upon road development and traffic control. One of the major problems of bus operations has been the inability to run on established schedules, in large part because of tremendous traffic congestion, particularly at rush hours. It has been noted that traffic control in Lagos is ineffective. A six-man detachment from the metropolitan police assigned to the Lagos city treasurer's office compose the total enforcement staff for this purpose. Moreover, tradeswomen and market stalls encroach upon sidewalks and roadways, forcing pedestrians into the streets. As these activities provide the livelihood for a great number of people in Lagos, traffic control is closely contingent upon provision of adequate sidewalk and market spaces throughout the central city. Without this, enforcement efforts have only solidified the intransigent attitudes of the public toward local government.

While the Lagos City Council and district councils in the Western Region are responsible for local street construction and maintenance, major bridges and primary roads are constructed by the federal Ministry of Works, while the regional government provides secondary roads. At present, Carter Bridge provides only four lanes between Lagos Island and the mainland, and there are two major road routes running north-south in the urban area, and one leading to Apapa. Construction of a second bridge got under way in 1966.

Appraisal of the Transportation Facilities

While roughly 90 per cent of the metropolitan population has ultimate access to public transport routes for the longer intraurban journeys, the routes do not penetrate the heart of the principal city, nor is there a detailed local network in the urban area. Public transport traverses Lagos Island and the urban complex on the major roads only, primarily on a north-south axis. The vertical orientation of transportation routes creates serious problems in the outer portions of the urban complex, where development is of necessity spreading out at greater distances from the main roads.   Residents who live off the main roads must walk considerable distances in order to use mass transportation.

The total number of municipal and private buses--about 230--is insufficient for traffic demand.   The obvious results are overcrowding, discomfort, poor scheduling, and slow speed, particularly during the peak hours, when people are packed in the buses, sardinelike, pushing and being pushed after waiting for long periods of time.   Long journeys to work are the rule, more than two hours each way for thousands of people.   A trip from Suru-Lere to Apapa, only a few miles, can take two hours during the morning peak period.   Moreover, in some cases, 10 to 15 per cent of the family budget is spent on transport fares.   Delays are encountered in every form of goods and passenger movement in Lagos.   Pedestrian and motor vehicle accidents occur with high frequency due to lack of traffic lights, safety islands, and guard rails, as well as to scant prosecution of driving violations.   Over 50 per cent of all traffic fatalities in Lagos are pedestrians or cyclists.

While the municipal bus services could be vastly improved, it is clear that demands cannot be met merely by increasing the number of buses and improving their operations.   It is highly doubtful that many more buses could be accommodated on present roads, even with substantial improvement in traffic control.   LCTS improvements seem to have been premised on the increase of its fleet, to which more than thirty buses were added in 1965-66.   As it has now been revealed through the proceedings of the Saville Commission of Inquiry (1966), the decision to expand the fleet was more influenced by opportunities for financial gain then by a desire to improve the transport service.

In addition to deficiencies in the transportation infrastructure, there is very little coordination among the existing modes of transportation as to schedules or routes.   Each agency operates with a considerable degree of autonomy and tends to take a narrow view of the transport needs of Lagos, depending upon its own responsibilities.   Although the federal government plays a major role, its transportation activities are fragmented among the Nigerian Railway Corporation, the Ministry of Transport, the Ministry of Works, the Inland Waterways Board, and--until 1966--the Ministry of Lagos Affairs.   The only recent effort to bring about service

changes has come from an agency that has no direct responsibility for transportation: the Ministry of Labor and Social
Services. This was a result of the protests by the labor
unions, culminating in a nation-wide strike in 1964, during
which the demand for higher wages was linked to transport
fares and difficult journies to work. As a result of these
pressures, the Ministry of Labor and Social Service has
requested the Lagos City Transport Service and private employers to work out a scheme for special passes at reduced
rates for low-income workers. * The argument is made
that there are valid economic and social reasons for de-
parting from the principle of self-financing for journies to
work, given low wages and rising costs of living.

Many of the people in Lagos feel that transportation
deficiencies are a serious grievance. Other pressures
brought to bear have been continual criticism of the LCTS
by the minority faction in the Lagos City Council and by the
press. These have played a part in bringing about the
creation of the Lagos City Transport Board and inquiries
into LCTS management.

Planning and Capital Expansion

There are no articulated government plans for transportation development in the Lagos urban area. Without general policies pertaining to the various transportation modes
and relating them to land-use patterns and without planned
commitment of funds, inertia prevails. Significant improvements in the system are not taking place. New housing and
industrial parks have been created in Lagos without corresponding extensions in transportation services, apart from
ad hoc extensions of already crowded bus lines into the major
settlement areas.

---

* There has been established the Working Committee on the
Provision of Cheap Transport for Workers. The Federal
Office of Statistics is now processing and evaluating data as-
sembled from a research questionnaire on the subject. Alternatives under consideration include:

1. Discount tickets to be used during specified hours of
the day; or

The case for transportation planning and coordinated
policy-making for Lagos was made, however, by the United
Nations survey in 1962. The assistance team included a
transportation expert who concluded that the existing pattern
of transport in Lagos inhibits efficient movement of people
and goods and thus applies a brake on economic expansion.
A transportation master plan covering twenty years or more
was suggested as the basis for improvement. The team
recommended that the plan should consist of component projects that could be implemented sequentially or simultaneously as money and opportunity permit. On the assumption
that buses will become less and less able to cope with Lagos
passenger traffic because of high daytime density in the central business district and extreme peaks of travel, a public
rapid transit system was proposed.

A monorail system was envisaged, which would carry
approximately 15,000 passengers per day in each direction on
four-car trains running at two-minute headways. Choice between a suspended or supported type of monorail would depend upon results of comparative economic and technical
studies. The construction costs were estimated at Ⱡ5 million,
exclusive of clearance and acquisition of rights of way.
Maintenance and operating costs are estimated at Ⱡ350,000
per year. Financing of construction would be by foreign
loan at 7 per cent per year, of which amortization could be
completed in seventeen years, according to the survey, if
the fares were 6d. per ride and if the monorail carried one-
third of Lagos' passenger movement. No operating subsidies
were contemplated.

---

2. Blue tickets entitling holders to minimum fares at any
time they utilize public transport facilities.

Unless the privilege is granted only to workers and not
their families, a serious inequity would result by comparison
to other segments of the population (e. g. , the unemployed,
and traders). Following the same line of argument, the
first method would appear more just than the second, in that
it subsidizes the journey to work per se rather than a group
of persons.

With single-track loops at both ends, the proposed route would start from Yaba, and extend to Iddo, where it would cross the lagoon to Lagos Island (see Map 1). Alternative routings within the city were suggested. The monorail system would not operate outside of the city limits, but three other developments were recommended as complements of the system. First, it was suggested that feeder buses connect with the monorail network. Second, commuter train services to Apapa, which would not be served by monorail, would be improved by the addition of tracks allowing operating of four trains per hour. Third, it was suggested that the extensive lagoon system in and around Lagos be utilized for rapid public transport by hydrofoil boats. While this service could be undertaken profitably by private ferry companies, according to the U. N. team, dredging and the provision of harbor facilities would have to be undertaken at government expense.

The city council has not been unaffected by the U. N. survey. It recommended many of the major suggestions in the U. N. survey--coordination of metropolitan transport, establishment of a metropolitan transport authority, road improvement, etc.--in its submission to the Saville Commission.

A supplementary survey of Lagos was made by the Allweg Company of Germany, which proposed that it could undertake the monorail project, either on its own or in collaboration with the Lagos City Council or Ministry of Lagos Affairs. The details of the Allweg proposals are not available but the suggested routing would be far longer than that proposed in the U. N. survey. It would serve the entire urban complex, running northward from Lagos Island approximately 14 miles through Iddo, Ebute-Metta, Yaba, Mushin, and Oshodi to Ikeja. A branch route of 5 miles would serve Apapa.

Although both monorail plans have been seriously considered by the Ministry of Lagos Affairs and the government, there is little indication that either of them will be implemented in the next few years. If action is taken on them, the initial stages of consultation and policy-making would take place within the Ministries of Works, Internal Affairs, and Transport and the Lagos City Council, including the affiliate agencies--the Lagos City Transport Service and Lagos

Executive Development Board. The Ministry of Works would
be involved in project design, and the Ministry of Finance
in foreign loan negotiations and management. Operation of
the monorail would be by the LCTS according to present policies unless technical factors make it impracticable. (The
United Nations survey proposed that the suggested metropolitan development agency take over all transportation planning and operations of rapid transit.)

The reasons for lack of action taken on the proposals
to date are several: (1) deficiency of financial resources on
the part of the government; (2) lack of expertise that could
be utilized to dramatize the importance of the proposal and
to establish the operational machinery for implementing it;
(3) bus interests that are opposed to a rapid transit system;
and (4) uncertainty as to the suitability of monorail relative
to other modes.

The United Nations team also studied and made proposals on street and highway capacity in Lagos, and a team
of private consultants, Hillyer and Whiting, had undertaken
a highway survey for the Ministry of Lagos Affairs in 1960.
New facilities proposed by the U. N. team included: an L-
shaped axial motorway from Agege through Lagos Island to
Victoria Island; six new lanes of bridges to the mainland by
1965, and twenty by 1980; a four-lane road with limited
access, which would parallel the motorway going north; and
adequate parking space and better traffic control. At present, construction of a second bridge to the mainland is underway by the Ministry of Works with German financial and
technical assistance.

It is clear that if the serious deficiencies of the
transportation system in Lagos are to be reduced, the federal government will have to take the initiative to commit
itself to large-scale investment, which it has as yet not
been willing to do. A comprehensive planning effort must
be undertaken to establish priorities among the various
modes of improvement and to weigh the costs and benefits
of various projects, given the present resources and priorities of the National Development Plan. Transportation
must compete, of course, with water, sewage, and housing
for scarce federal resources and foreign assistance programs in Lagos.

PUBLIC HOUSING PROGRAMS

There are two public agencies in the urban area that construct public housing and develop housing sites: the Lagos Executive Development Board (LEDB), which operates exclusively within the federal territory; and the Western Nigeria Housing Corporation (WNHC), which operates throughout the Western Region. The bulk of the regional corporation's projects have been located in Ibadan and Ikeja, the latter being within the Lagos metropolitan area.

The Lagos Executive Development Board, which was described in Chapter 4, is a multipurpose agency charged with public housing and specialized public works related to housing, as well as land-use planning and control. Several of the board's divisions are involved in the housing programs, including town planning, engineering, land survey, finance, architecture, and estate management. It is empowered to undertake compulsory purchase of land, to enter into contracts for leasing and sale of land, as well as to construct housing. The board has been responsible to the Ministry of Lagos Affairs, which approved selection of its high ranking officials, arranged for federal loans or grants, and assigned specific tasks to it. The ministry retained responsibility for reclaiming and developing land, tasks that the LEDB executed on a contractual basis. In 1966, the ministerial duties with respect to housing and land development in Lagos were transferred to the Ministry of Works and Housing.

The Western Nigeria Housing Corporation, established in 1958 by the regional government with an expressed policy purpose to stimulate home ownership, develops open land areas and builds both housing and industrial estates* for freehold and leasehold. The corporation also grants long-term low-interest mortgage loans and manages a savings scheme.

The corporation is managed by a board consisting of a chairman, two executive directors, and between four and

---

* Housing estates are residential subdivisions, while industrial estates approximate the industrial park in American usage.

six other members appointed by the regional government. In
1962, the total number of employees of the housing corporation was 92. Executive control of its day-to-day activities
is exercised by the general manager, who is responsible to
the chairman of the board. The internal organization of the
corporation consists of an administration and legal department, with 40 employees; an estates department, with 13;
an engineering and architectural department, with 23; and
the accounts department, with 16. Top-level posts are
filled by the board on the basis of prescribed qualifications,
but political party affiliation has important influence on the
choices.

The housing corporation operates with a considerable degree of autonomy, although it is formally responsible
to the Ministry of Lands and Housing of the regional government and to some degree is dependent upon the Ministry of
Finance. The corporation does consult informally with the
LEDB and the Ikeja Town Planning Authority with respect
to its operations in the Lagos urban area. In addition, it
maintains liaison with several federal agencies, including
Lagos Water Supply, the Electricity Corporation of Nigeria,
and the Posts and Telegraph Department of the Ministry of
Communications, in order to ensure provision of services
for its developments.

In addition to the LEDB and Western Nigeria Housing
Corporation, there are two federal agencies involved in
housing activities throughout Nigeria, and to some extent
within the Lagos urban area: the Nigerian Building Society
and the African Staff Housing Fund. The latter engages in
mortgage lending to civil servants, and its operation requires considerable government investment and interest
subsidies. The loans of up to £4,000 that are extended by
it are frequently used for construction of relatively expensive houses.

The Nigerian Building Society is jointly owned and
controlled by the federal government, the Eastern Region
government, and the Commonwealth Development Corporation, a foreign assistance agency. It is, in theory, an
aided savings and loan institution in the housing finance market. Its initial capitalization, received from the three parti-
cipating agents, is supplemented by loans from both the federal government and the Commonwealth Development

Corporation.   The private deposits received by the society (on which it pays 8. 5 per cent interest), are a small part of its resources, amounting in 1962 to only Ł60, 000.   About 60 per cent of its gross profits are returned to the federal government in taxes and dividends.

Housing Programs in Lagos

Construction activities in Lagos by the Western Nigeria Housing Corporation and the LEDB have been small scale to date.

The housing corporation had constructed 137 houses for sale in the urban area by 1962, four years after its creation. *   These are on a 450-acre residential section of the Ikeja estate.   The houses range in price from Ł1, 750 to Ł4, 330.   In addition, prepared building plots in the estate are sold by the corporation, and fifteen-year mortgage loans at 7 per cent annual interest are extended to private builders, who may use either plots developed privately or plots sold by the corporation.   Depositors in the corporation's savings program are given priorities for its mortgages.

The housing corporation has also developed and leased industrial sites on some 300 acres of the same estate.   It has constructed roads, made a financial contribution to Lagos Water Supply for extension of water mains, and planned an industrial-waste treatment plant on the estate. Moreover, the corporation has acquired and cleared land for a similar estate at Ajeromi, in the western segment of the Lagos metropolitan area.

The Western Nigeria Housing Corporation operates at a profit. **   Its houses, plots, and mortgages are offered

---

* Later figures were not available to the authors.

** For example, its net operating profit was Ł61, 531 in 1962, of which Ł47, 629 was derived from operations at Ikeja.   After repayment of loan capital, that year's net surplus was Ł37, 886.

at above cost, although the cost of houses constructed by it frequently exceeds the legal minimum for them. Its mortgage program requires a down payment of at least 20 per cent of the total cost of the house constructed.

The corporation depends on loans from the Western Region government (Ministry of Lands and Housing) for its capital financing. Its cumulative capital loans account in 1962 stood at ₺1,387,000. These loans are repaid with interest out of profits. In addition, it had received equity capital of ₺500,000.

The Lagos Executive Development Board has undertaken several types of housing-related programs in the urban area, including slum clearance, construction of houses for rent, construction of houses for sale, preparation of building sites for sale and subdivision development. The projects have varied in both purpose and origin, some having been initiated by the federal government--such as the Suru-Lere schemes, which are the only instances of subsidized publicly built housing in Lagos.

The Suru-Lere settlement is entirely composed of several LEDB housing developments: rehousing estates I, II, III, and III-A; Lagos low-income housing scheme; and freehold housing schemes. Suru-Lere rehousing estates I, II, and III were designed to accommodate families displaced by slum clearance in central Lagos, while III-A was to rehouse refugees from a fire in central Lagos. In these estates, the LEDB has built more than 2,000 houses of various types with capital grants from the federal government. Two, three, or four-room, single-story houses with kitchen, shower, and water closet have been constructed, each with piped water supply, water-borne sewage, and electricity. Some one-room houses with access to sanitary facilities have also been built. These single-family homes are supplemented by two-story buildings of two- or three-room flats, each with a kitchen and bathroom. Efforts were made in these schemes to ensure maximum density consistent with construction cost differentials. Since there is an estimated cost differential of ₺90 per room between a single-story house (₺310 per room) and a two-story house (₺400 per room), a compromise between economizing on land and on construction costs was chosen--grouping both types of houses in the estates. All of the dwellings in the rehousing estates are owned and rented by the LEDB at approximately Ł1:5/- per month per room. The difference between this figure and an economic rent of roughly Ł2:10/- is covered by federal subsidy.

The Lagos low-income-housing scheme, which was initiated by the federal government in 1955, consists of 1,300 houses to accommodate low-income workers. The net estimated cost of this project was Ł1.1 million. The houses are rented to tenants who fulfill specific eligibility requirements: they have incomes under Ł300 per year; they have been in continuous employment for at least five years; and they have at least ten years' residence in Lagos at the time of application. When the program commenced, some 4,400 applications were received for the 1,300 houses. A point system of priorities was developed and awards were determined on the basis of the length of continuous employment, length of residence in Lagos, and the size of family in relation to existing living conditions of the applicant. Although the economic rent per room per month in these houses is roughly Ł2:10/-, occupants pay 16s. 6d. inclusive of tax rates. The difference is subsidized by a grant from the Ministry of Lagos Affairs spread over forty years. This development has been managed by a special committee appointed by the minister of Lagos affairs.

The rest of Suru-Lere is composed of several freehold subdivisions. The Itire Road estates, for example, cover some 185 acres, on which a neighborhood center and 670 residential building plots were developed by the LEDB. These are sold at a profit to private individuals who build for themselves. The LEDB adds a 15 per cent (or higher) development charge to the costs of the prepared sites in computing the price. Legal provisions require that only houses of specified values and types be constructed on these plots.

Finally, the LEDB has built freehold houses for sale. Initial financing of this type of construction is derived from loans from commercial banks, the federal government, and the Commonwealth Development Corporation, each of which must be approved by the minister.* These houses have been sold at a substantial profit at prices ranging from Ł1,870 to Ł5,500. Mortgage loans covering up to 80 per cent of the total value of the houses are extended to the purchasers at 7 per cent annual interest. While the maximum period for repayment is twenty-five years, the average amortization period is fifteen years. The mortgage loans are guaranteed by the Nigerian Building Society, except for senior civil servants, for whom the federal government guarantees loans.

The total number of houses built and being built by the LEDB is approximately 4,000 for rent under the low-income and rehousing schemes, plus approximately 1,200 for sale. In addition, the LEDB has acquired and cleared the land; constructed roads, drains, and street lights; and arranged for provision of basic services in the estates.

Other projects of the LEDB include the Apapa estate, where 1,000 acres of land have been developed for industrial as well as high- and low-density residential uses. Begun in 1950, this project has required capital expenditure of approximately Ł2.5 million, financed by loans from the Commonwealth Development Corporation and the federal government.** The LEDB has also carried out land reclamation and redevelopment operations at Ikoyi and on Victoria Island and is undertaking development of another industrial estate in the Ijora area. Finally, the LEDB has undertaken a slum-clearance project in central Lagos, which is discussed below.

Apart from the subsidized rental housing provided at Suru-Lere, the projects of the LEDB are profit-making and serve middle-income groups. Even the subsidized housing

---

* The only instance of foreign assistance for housing in Lagos is that of low-interest medium-term loans totaling Ł1.2 million made to the LEDB by the Commonwealth Development Corporation.

** The plots for industrial use are leased at Ł350 to Ł450 per acre per year. Plots for low-density residential use are leased at Ł120 to Ł170 per acre per year and those for high-density residential use, at Ł75 per acre per year.

is, in fact, too expensive for the lowest-income groups in the urban area and the new migrants are not eligible for the low-income units. While legal provisions limit the value of houses built on plots purchased from the LEDB and require that they be owner occupied, these regulations are frequently transgressed. Given the extremely high unsatisfied demand for housing in Lagos, it has proved almost impossible to control subletting and reselling of LEDB houses and plots at substantial private profits.

In any case, the pace of construction by the Western Nigeria Housing Corporation and the LEDB is very slow in relation to housing deficiencies. Applying a standard (defined by the LEDB) of two persons per room in residential dwelling units, in July, 1964, there was an aggregate shortage of accommodation for 93,400 people in the City of Lagos alone. As there are tremendous diversities between occupational density in high-income and low-income residential areas, it is realistic to estimate that over 100,000 people should be accommodated by new dwelling space to reduce overcrowding.* This would require approximately 50,000 rooms or 11,000-12,000 dwelling units of an average 4.7 rooms each (the present average in the city). Thus, to overcome the present housing shortage in twenty years, at least 600 houses a year must be built. Furthermore, to keep up with present rates of growth, approximately 4,000 new dwelling units per year must be constructed. In addition, approximately 1,900 dwelling units per year will be required to replace obsolete or deteriorating housing. Hence, a modest target to overcome housing shortages, replace dilapidated units, and accommodate new growth is construction of 6,500 dwelling units per year. By comparison the actual construction rate between 1961 and 1964 by both public and private parties was approximately 1,100 dwelling units per year.

---

* According to the records of the Lagos City Council, there are an average of 4.7 rooms and 11 persons per dwelling unit in Lagos. As occupancy rates are far lower than this average in the low-density sections of the city, conditions in high-density sections are far more severe than the average figures would indicate. There are no statistics on sanitary and other facilities, but it is clear that these are severely deficient in low-income units.

These figures relate only to the City of Lagos. It is clear that the requirements of the Western Region portion of the urban area are as great, if not greater. The rate of population growth in this section is far higher and both public and private building activities have been less vigorous than those in the city. The annual construction target recommended by the United Nations assistance team however was 6, 000 dwelling units per year for the entire metropolitan area.

Demands for expansion of government activities in the housing field have been increasing rapidly, particularly among workers and trade unions, which are articulating protests about the dearth and costs of adequate housing. * The trade unions have urged their case through the press, the radio, and, above all, in the general strike of 1964. It was largely in response to these demands that the new Ministry of Housing was created in 1964. This was subsequently merged with the Ministry of Works, which in conjunction with the Lagos Executive Development Board, has prepared a new program for expanded public housing activities to meet the demands of low-income workers in Lagos.

Housing Planning for Lagos

There has been to date no comprehensive planning for housing improvement in Lagos, although some construction targets have been articulated by the LEDB. The LEDB is neither staffed nor organized for comprehensive planning efforts, which in any case would require cooperation between the federal and regional governments. The United Nations team recommended that a metropolitan development authority, with jurisdiction over the entire urban area, be given responsibility to develop priorities for housing and to prepare a comprehensive land-use and housing plan. At present, however, these functions are the responsibility of the LEDB, the federal housing ministry, and the Western Region Ministry of Lands and Housing.

----

* On the other hand, the recently organized House Owners-Renters Association opposes rent control and large-scale expansion of public housing.

While the National Development Plan for 1962-68 includes general targets for investment in housing, it does not formulate operational programs. The federal housing program for Lagos (referred to as the Metropolitan Housing Scheme) states that 24,000 new housing units are required in the city to prevent deterioration of already overcrowded housing conditions and specifies that 60 per cent of these units should be available for low-income groups, 30 per cent for middle-income groups, and 10 per cent for upper-income groups. While it recognizes that the housing problem is closely related to the land problem, it does not raise the issue of utilizing land outside the city limits. It proposes total direct investment in housing during the plan period of some Ł15 million, to be supplemented by profits of sales and leases, and contributions from the Nigerian Building Society and the African Staff Housing Fund. Most of the suggested programs would be executed by the LEDB. The proposals include land reclamation and land development in Yaba, Victoria Island, and Suru-Lere; mass production of cheap shell houses for sale at economic prices; and mortgage financing for middle-income groups at unsubsidized rates.

The feasibility of this section of the plan cannot be evaluated because the proposals do not specify magnitude of construction or specific costs. In any case, the investment proposed is unlikely to produce anything close to construction of 24,000 dwelling units envisaged under the Metropolitan Housing Scheme in the plan period.

An attempt to spell out parts of the Metropolitan Housing Scheme has been made by the new housing ministry, which prepared a plan in 1965 calling for immediate expenditure of Ł1.38 million for low-income housing to accommodate about 11,000 persons in the next few years. In spite of the political upheavals in 1966 while this plan was under consideration, it has been approved by the military government and is now to be executed by the Lagos Executive Development Board. Additional public housing activity has been started in a new slum-clearance sector in neighborhoods affected by the second mainland bridge from Lagos Island, which is under construction. These developments may be viewed as partial implementation of the general proposals in the national plan, but the catalyst for them was the trade union protests generated in mid-1964.

Administrative Problems

The federal government is at the heart of public housing activities within the City of Lagos.   Over half of the total
capital resources of the Lagos Executive Development Board
up to March, 1963, were obtained from that government.
The source of the capital account up to that time breaks down
as follows:

Loans	Ꝉ 3, 645, 099
Nigerian federal government	2, 177, 000
Commonwealth Development Corp.	1, 208, 099
Bank of West Africa Ltd.	260, 000
Grants (Nigerian federal government)	5, 143, 124
Other sources (LEDB income from sales, rents, and mortgages)	4, 114, 373
Total	Ꝉ12, 903, 597

The Ministry of Lagos Affairs controlled the allocation of all
public land utilized by the LEDB and approved its project
plans.   In the housing field, the LEDB is essentially an implementing agent for the federal authorities, henceforth for
the housing ministry.

Outside the city limits, housing activities of the Western Nigeria Housing Corporation are initiated, financed, and
approved by the regional government.   There is neither formal machinery nor informal tendency for cooperation between
the two governments or between the LEDB and the Western
Nigeria Housing Corporation.   There is little doubt that the
progress of public housing is retarded by the fact that the
bulk of funds available for this purpose is allocated to the
Lagos Executive Development Board, which cannot operate
outside the city limits, while the bulk of land available at
reasonable costs lies in the Western Region portion of the
metropolitan area.   This anomaly implies that either the
LEDB should be allowed to extend its operations into regional territory (as has been done by Lagos Water Supply
and the Lagos City Transport Service), or the investment
funds allocated by the regional government to the Western
Nigeria Housing Corporation should be increased significantly,

perhaps with the aid of federal grants to the region. The dysfunction between land control and financial ability demonstrates the importance of effective intergovernmental relationships to tackle metropolitan problems, be they within a metropolitan organization or between existing organizations.

The effectiveness and scope of public housing programs in Lagos has been limited by several other problems. First, there is a severe shortage of technical staff in the housing field. Second, federal financial regulations place a ceiling on the activities of the LEDB. Bond issues could increase its ability to engage in profitable projects, such as sales of developed plots and houses, which would step up its accumulation of capital. Many viable LEDB projects are delayed by insufficient initial capitalization from the federal government. And the exercise of financial controls by the ministry has on some occasions distorted the housing priorities that had been determined primarily from technical and functional points of view. Third, the activities of the LEDB do not directly benefit those income and social groups in greatest need of housing; nor does it appear that the LEDB has considered many alternatives of shelter (other than conventional flats and houses) that might be provided for migrants and low-income groups.

Finally, the attempts to improve housing conditions in Lagos are fraught with the financial and technical problems found in most rapidly growing urban areas in developing nations: high land costs and uncontrolled speculation in land; incomplete registration of land titles and an extremely complex land market; limited financial market and private savings; small proportions of public investment capital allocated to social infrastructure; and the absence of a large-scale building industry. The growing public demand for action on the housing front and increasing health hazards underscore needs to tackle these problems in the near future.

Slum Clearance

All of the problems with which housing programs in Lagos are beset are illustrated by the central Lagos slum-clearance project. The scheme, which was designed by the federal government in 1951 and begun two years later, aimed to clear and redevelop 70 acres in the densely populated, western end of Lagos Island, which contained over 30,000 persons. While the site was a slum by European standards of overcrowding and sanitary conditions, most of its inhabitants had lived there for several generations in large compounds with and near other members of their extended families. The kin groups functioned as close-knit social and economic units. [2]

The Lagos Executive Development Board was assigned responsibility for executing the project. After acquiring the land by compulsory purchase, it was to replan the area; to construct roads and public areas; and to develop new residential plots for resale at economic prices. The whole undertaking was to be self-financing in the long run, according to project plans. A capital outlay of Ł3 million was to be recovered from sales of prepared sites.

Resistance of the inhabitants to acquisition of their land was vigorous and occasionally violent. Under these pressures, the government made several compromises in the project plans. It extended to the original owners first options on repurchase of their plots, at 120 per cent of the public acquisition cost. In the meantime, they were to be rehoused at Suru-Lere.

At this stage, the project plans were unrealistic and internally inconsistent. First, after roads, open spaces, and commercial plots were provided, there would not be enough residential land to accommodate all the original owners on separate plots. Second, most of the original owners could not afford to buy back the land and build new homes on it. Titles to the land were unregistered and frequently vested in large families rather than individuals, rendering allocation of compensation and negotiations for repurchase extremely complex. The obligation to offer the plots in turn to multiple claimants could delay sales practically indefinitely. Third, revisions of the plan to provide for many small plots violated the original planning concepts for improving land use in the area. Fourth, housing at Suru-Lere was unsatisfactory to most residents of central Lagos, as the move would overturn social and economic ways of life and increase the cost of living. In any case, the number of houses built at Suru-Lere could not accommodate half the people who were to be displaced. People who did move to Suru-Lere were separated from their extended family and from the markets for their goods and services. That central

Lagos had been not only their home but also their work area was overlooked by the planners. Fifth, under the agreement with the original owners it would be impossible for the scheme to pay for itself, although the assumption of self-financing was maintained even in the National Development Plan of 1962-68.

As a result, the slum-clearance work ground to a halt. By 1962, seven years after the start of the project, the LEDB had cleared 25 of the 70 acres, having displaced 11,000 persons and removed hundreds of small shops and market stalls. Of these 25 acres, many have lain vacant; the LEDB has permitted roughly 400 temporary shops and stalls to be put up on them, ironically often by the very people who were there originally. About 4 acres have been rebuilt, and construction has been started on another acre. In addition, 5 acres have been resold but not built upon, and over 8 acres have been used for roads and public space.

While some modern urban facilities, such as the Bristol Hotel, several office buildings, and Tinubu Square, have risen in the cleared area, the city's housing plant has been reduced by the project. By 1962, Ł3.5 million had been spent and the project was bankrupt. The United Nations assistance team estimated that over Ł5 million more would be required to complete work on the 70 acres. Income from plot sales has been negligible, for most of the former owners have not applied for repurchase, and some of those who did make deposits on the land cannot now complete payment.* Neither the LEDB nor the former owners are financed to undertake rebuilding, and other prospective buyers are blocked by the option agreements. In the meantime, the subsidies to housing in Suru-Lere have become a controversial burden on the federal budget, far higher than expected.

The United Nations assistance team recommended that the government take one of two alternative steps to break the stalemate. It could abandon plans for clearance of the

---

* The town planning law was amended in 1960 to authorize the LEDB to return deposits to those people who refuse or are unable to complete repurchase.

remaining 45 acres (perhaps initiating an aided rehabilitation program). On the other hand, the team concluded, if the government wishes to proceed, the scheme must be replanned and refinanced, and the rights of redemption of the former owners eliminated, with appropriate compensation.

The difficulties encountered in this effort are attributable to errors and gaps in planning on the one hand, inadequate financing on the other. The original project plans were not designed in terms of general priorities for housing and were not technically feasible. Nor were the side effects of the work--the various costs and benefits generated--considered. This was not primarily the fault of the LEDB staff, which was responsible for execution of the project, but rather of the general shortage of experienced project planners in the federal government and absence of general housing and development strategies and policies. Moreover, the last-minute responses of the government to protests of the citizenry were not consistent with reality or the project goals. Considering the inherent obstacles, the LEDB performed extremely well in completing such work as it did. Finally, Western prototypes and standards underlay the project design while the economic and social characteristics of the population in Lagos demand adaptation of program approaches (the project was initiated prior to independence). Accommodations for extended families, group shelters for migrants, aided rehabilitation and self-building, and development of residential neighborhoods containing market places and work centers are examples of potentially constructive approaches. There has been a great deal of private "installment" construction in Nigeria whereby a family purchases building materials gradually. Credit, technical assistance, and mass production of parts could expand this traditional sector of home building considerably.

EDUCATION

According to the Constitution of the Nigerian federation, education is a concurrent subject for which both the federal and regional governments are responsible. Federal activity in education has been directed to higher and specialized institutions, except in the Federal Territory of Lagos, where the national government has primary responsibility for elementary and secondary schools. There, it has delegated several education responsibilities to the Lagos City Council and its education department.

Historically, education has been in large part a private function in Nigeria. Traditionally a family responsibility, education was formalized and offered by voluntary agencies and religious missions after colonial contact. Most schools are still owned and operated by private organizations but now with subsidies from the government. While an effort is being made to develop government schools, most existing schools in the Lagos area were mission-started, are mission-run, and are state-supported. These privately owned schools are an integral part of the public education system for which the government defines standards, trains teachers, inspects classroom activities, awards diplomas, and reimburses costs.

There are five elementary schools in the City of Lagos that were built by the federal government and are managed by the city education department. Attached to the teacher-training college at Suru-Lere, there is one elementary demonstration school that is run by the national government. The remaining elementary schools (over 95 per cent) are privately built and managed. All secondary schools in Lagos, except three that are operated by the federal ministry, are managed by private agencies but are state supported (see Table 4). In the remainder of the metropolitan area there are similar arrangements between the regional government, local authorities, and voluntary agencies.

The Nigerian education system in general is modeled on that of Great Britain (see Charts 3 and 4). After "infant" grades, the first type of school in the system is the elementary school of six grades. Elementary education in Lagos is free and is meant to be universal. There is no compulsory school attendance age for either boys or girls. Children may attend school without payment of tuition from age five to thirteen in the city, and from six to twelve in the Western Region. All children whose parents are residents of the area and who are properly registered may attend elementary school without payment of tuition. The curricula of the municipal and privately run (but publicly financed) schools are uniform. There is, however, a new group of primary schools (Corona Schools) that are similar to English "public schools"

TABLE 4

NUMBER OF SCHOOLS AND PUPILS[a] IN THE CITY OF LAGOS,
BY MANAGING AUTHORITY

Elementary Schools

	Federal Government	Local Authority	Private, Aided	Private, Unaided	Total
1958	1 (523)	1 (696)	76 (51,231)	21 (4,256)	99 (56,688)
1959	1 (645)	1 (676)	85 (61,972)	16 (2,936)	103 (66,320)
1960	1 (726)	3 (1,347)	95 (68,545)	13 (3,850)	112 (74,468)
1961	1 (811)	4 (2,352)	97 (75,247)	15 (3,370)	117 (81,780)
1962	1 (1,131)	5 (4,329)	98 (88,505)	16 (4,546)	120 (98,511)

Secondary Schools

	Federal Government	Private, Aided	Private, Unaided	Total
1958	2 (508)	14 (2,561)	3 (1,522)	19 (4,591)
1959	2 (581)	13 (2,580)	3 (1,643)	18 (4,804)
1960	2 (568)	24 (3,780)	3 (1,366)	29 (5,714)
1961	2 (644)	27 (3,931)	10 (2,517)	39 (7,092)
1962	3 (1,075)	27 (4,559)	14 (4,424)	44 (10,058)

a Number of pupils appears in parentheses.
Source: Ministry of Education, 1964.

CHART 3

THE EDUCATIONAL SYSTEM: FEDERAL TERRITORY

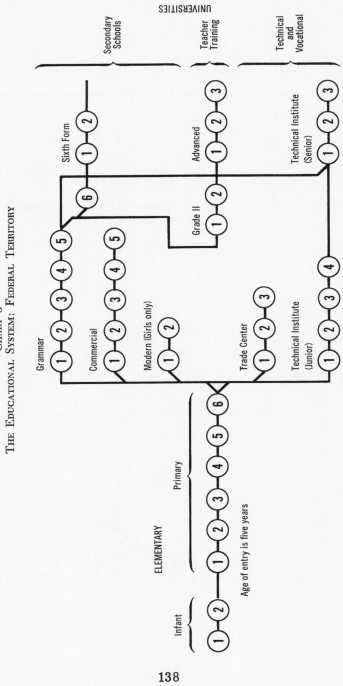

138

CHART 4
THE EDUCATIONAL SYSTEM: WESTERN REGION

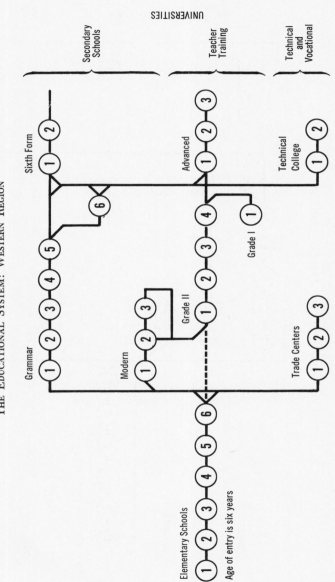

139

(i.e., "private," in American usage) and remain outside the public education system. Developed to meet the demands of expatriate students, these schools are also patronized by upper-income Africans. They are not financed or supported in any way by the state and have unique curricula.

Second, there are "modern" schools in Nigeria, which fall between elementary and secondary grammar schools. These provide postelementary terminal training for students who are not expected to enter institutions of higher learning. There are no separate modern schools within the city limits, but attached to elementary schools there are modern classes that provide two-year programs preparatory to some vocations. Designed mainly for girls, they lay the foundation for training in nursing, dress-making, beauty culture, etc. There are separate modern schools in the Western Region that provide three-year programs for both boys and girls.

Third, there is one trade center in the Lagos urban area. Located at Yaba, it provides a two-year training program in several trades and crafts, such as plumbing, masonry, painting, etc.

Fourth, there are three types of secondary schools in the urban area. The first is the secondary grammar school, which is the backbone of the secondary education system. Patterned after the English grammar school, it provides education with a literary orientation, prepares students for university and professional training, and is a terminal institution for the greater number of pupils. Most of the secondary grammar schools offer five years. At the end of this course the secondary "school-leaving certificate" (the Cambridge School Leaving Certificate or the West African School Certificate) is awarded on the basis of examinations. In addition, a few of these schools offer two extra years of education beyond the certificate, which are preparatory to university work. The second type consists of secondary commercial schools in the urban area, which provide a five-year basic course and an additional two-year "senior phase." They offer instruction in bookkeeping, accounting, typing, shorthand, etc. It is the policy of the government to encourage growth of these schools in order to expand vocational education to meet the needs of rapidly growing industry and commerce. Finally, there are secondary comprehensive

schools, which combine the facilities of a secondary grammar school and technical training. There are two of these in
the federal territory; one is wholly state-managed (the Yaba
College of Technology), and the other (St. Finbarr's) is run
by a Roman Catholic agency with state support. These
schools are leaning more toward technical than literary education and provide training in such fields as draftsmanship,
elementary engineering, and surveying.

Government Education Authorities in the City

The federal minister of education is responsible for
education policy in Lagos. Under his political leadership
the permanent secretary is administrative director of the
Ministry of Education as well as chief adviser to the government on education. Immediately subordinate to him are
the administrative senior secretary, the adviser on secondary and postsecondary education, and the adviser on
teacher training. The personnel of the ministry are gov-
erned by Nigerian civil service regulations and are recruited by the Nigeria Public Service Commission. A
separate section of the federal budget is devoted to the
Ministry of Education.

Elementary and secondary school matters are dealt
with by the department under the management of the senior
secretary for administration. Its functions with respect to
elementary education include supervision of the Lagos City
Council education department, extension of grants to the
city education department, definition of curricula and educational standards; registration of pupils and teachers in
the federal territory; inspection of schools; and management
of the few special federal educational institutions. Other
elementary school-related duties have been delegated to the
city council. The main function of the ministry in elementary education is school finance; grants for municipal and
voluntary agency schools are channeled by it through the
Lagos City Council.

The ministry is fully responsible for the management
and operation of secondary schools in the city. It provides
total support of secondary schools directly, supervises their
operations, and acquires sites for school construction. Under the administrative senior secretary in the ministry are

two chief education officers concerned with secondary schools in Lagos—one responsible for operations, and the other, for development and construction.

Responsibility for the operation and management of elementary schools within the city has been delegated to the Lagos City Council. For these purposes the council has constituted an education committee (a regular working committee of the council) and the city education department, which is managed by the chief education officer. This officer reports to the city council through the education committee.

While the Lagos City Council was appointed local education authority for elementary schools in 1961, the federal government maintains a close check on its activities in this field. The city education department is subject to supervision by the Lagos Education Committee, which is distinct and separate from the city council's education committee. The Lagos Education Committee is chaired by the federal minister of education and has two classes of members: those appointed by the permanent secretary of the ministry, and those appointed by the minister. The permanent secretary appoints one member as his representative and one woman education officer, while the minister appoints two members nominated by the Roman Catholic mission, two members nominated by the Christian Council of Nigeria, three members nominated by the Council of Moslem School Proprietors, three members nominated by the Lagos City Council, one member nominated by the Nigerian Union of Teachers, one member nominated by the African Communion Council. The committee has three types of function: (1) to advise and to report to the minister on any question of policy affecting education in the Lagos federal territory; (2) to perform any function assigned to it by the Lagos City Council; and (3) to carry out such other duties with which it is charged by law. It utilizes two major subcommittees: the Tenders Sub-Committee and Establishment of New Schools and Discipline of Teachers' Sub-Committee. The first issues directives for the expenditure of some grants-in-aid approved by the minister for authorized expenses of supported elementary schools. In this respect, it deals primarily with the purchase of books, paper, and other school materials. The second subcommittee makes recommendations to the full committee on applications for establishment of new schools and on cases involving discipline of teachers.

In effect, the Lagos Education Committee is a channel of communication linking the federal government, the city government, and the private interests for purposes of policy development and problem resolution relating to school operations. In addition, it has been charged by the federal Ministry of Education with responsibility for supervising Lagos schools and therefore is a watchdog over the city department of education.

The duties of the city education department are as follows: (1) to establish and to conduct such municipal schools as the minister may direct (thus far five elementary schools); (2) to assist voluntary schools as the minister may direct (by providing 30 per cent of recurrent costs from the city budget and administering federal 70-per cent grants); (3) to furnish the minister with advice, data, accounts, and estimates; (4) to ensure by inspection that the premises of every elementary school within its jurisdiction conform to standards prescribed (the federal government also undertakes inspection); and (5) to perform such other duties as are delegated to it, including school supervision and aid in establishing curricula. Subject to the approval of the minister, the Lagos City Council may establish nursery schools, schools for the handicapped, and facilities for recreation and physical training of pupils; may arrange for the provision of transportation for pupils; and may establish a school medical service. The council has undertaken most of these activities. Not only must it have approval of the minister of education, however, to establish a school or school service, but in addition the city elementary schools, like the voluntary schools, depend upon operating grants from the ministry for 100 per cent of capital costs and 70 per cent of operating costs.

There are growing demands from some quarters for the Lagos City Council to be made fully responsible for implementing education programs in the city by delegation from the ministry, which has considered turning over much of its regulatory and supervisory functions, although it would remain the primary source of school finance. Some of the pressure for further delegation arises from difficulties encountered under the present system of divided responsibility. For example, there is generally a delay in the appointment

of the Lagos Education Committee for months after each
election of a new city council. Further delays are encountered in ministerial approval of the council's annual estimates, with the result that much of the work of the Lagos
Education Committee has to be carried out without an established budgetary base for part of the year. Local and federal
inspection activities overlap. The chief education officer of
the city council is responsible for enrolling children, but
eligible pupils are registered by the federal government--
an arrangement that has produced delays in enrollment.

Jones and Lucas, in their examination of Lagos city
government in 1963, recommended that registration duties
be transferred to the chief education officer of the city. In
addition, they suggested that responsibility for secondary
education and the two federal officers dealing with it be
transferred to the city council, with compensating increases
in federal financial assistance. The advisability of further
delegation of powers to local government, however, must be
predicated upon the capabilities of that government, on
which some doubt is shed by current suspension and inquiries.

Education Authorities in the Western Region

Responsibility for education in Western Nigeria is
vested in the regional Ministry of Education, and is exercised by its officers in headquarters in Ibadan, as well as by
field inspectors in each district and by local education authorities. The minister of education, with concurrence of the
minister of local government, appoints either a district or
local council or a joint board of several councils as the local
education authority in each area of the region. Limited powers are then delegated to these local education authorities,
which, in the case of the Lagos metropolitan area, are the
district councils. Most activities performed by the councils
are subject to ministerial approval, often by both the minister of local government and the minister of education.

The duties and powers of the district councils, as
local education authorities, include reporting to the minister
of education on the school needs of the district; maintaining
existing elementary schools and modern schools; establishing
new public elementary schools and modern schools as the
minister may direct; assisting, with a prescribed percentage
grant, in the operating costs of voluntary agency schools;

establishing and maintaining teacher-training institutions as
directed by the minister; insuring by inspection that the
premises of every elementary and modern school situated
within its area conform to regionally prescribed standards;
and establishing, with the approval of the minister of education and the minister of local government, nursery schools,
schools for the disabled, trade centers, recreation facilities,
or pupil transport services. Thus, the functions delegated
to the district councils in the urban area closely parallel
those delegated by the federal government to the Lagos City
Council, with the exception that modern schools are included
in local authority responsibilities in the Western Region. In
both cases, local authorities are primarily implementors of
higher government decisions.

It is mandatory that each district council that has
been appointed a local education authority establish an education committee that includes not only members of the council
but also qualified members of the public, representatives of
teachers' organizations, and appointees of the minister who
represent the voluntary agencies that are proprietors of
schools in the district. The district education committee
in the Western Region resembles the special Lagos Education Committee in the city. The district council is required
to consult it before performing any function with respect to
education. School planning, school financing, regulation
and curricula establishment, and inspection are carried out
by the regional Ministry of Education. Local education activities are financed, for the most part, by annual grants from
this ministry.

In addition, local education advisers are assigned by
the ministry to supervise and advise each local education
authority. The minister may delegate to them his powers of
approval of local activities.

Regulation of Aided Schools

All schools in Lagos can only be opened or closed with
the approval of the minister of education, who acts on the
basis of recommendations by the Lagos Education Committee,
which investigates school plant and personnel. The minister
can enforce educational standards by ordering the plans of a
proposed school to be altered or instructing the education
committee to determine whether a given school should be

closed. If the education committee urges that a particular
school be closed, the minister may keep it open under his
supervision if he feels that closure will not serve the best
interest of the community. He can also initiate action for
compulsory acquisition if the proprietor of the school has
not complied with the terms of a capital grant.

The minister must approve the appointment of all
managers, proprietors, and boards of governors of aided
schools, and his inspectors can enter any part of the school
at all reasonable times and have access to all school personnel and school records.

The minister has authority to determine the school
calendar and the nature and content of the syllabus. In
general, it is accepted that directions and regulations concerning the secular instruction will not interfere with reasonable arrangements for religious instruction. At the
same time, religious schools may not refuse admission to
any pupil on religious grounds.

The educational standards applied to privately managed schools in Lagos appear to be effective and conscien-
tiously enforced, except in cases where they conflict with
other aspects of the public interest. This occurs when the
government is not satisfied with the management of a particular school but finds that in the short run there is no alternative school to accommodate its pupils.

Financial Decision-Making

Direct expenditures on elementary education in the
City of Lagos in a recent year are found in Table 5. The
figures reflect the overwhelming dominance of voluntary
agency schools. While the federal government is legally
responsible for reimbursement of 70 per cent of the recurrent expenditures, it actually disbursed Ł479,202 in that
fiscal year (roughly 57 per cent of the recurrent expenditures
of municipal and nonmunicipal schools).

In addition, during that year, the federal government
spent approximately Ł15,000 on the demonstration school at
Suru-Lere and made a total capital expenditure in new school
construction and acquisition of land for future works of
Ł126,279. Unaided private schools expended roughly Ł80,000.

TABLE 5

EXPENDITURE FOR ELEMENTARY EDUCATION
IN THE CITY OF LAGOS[a]

CLOSED ACCOUNTS	City Education Dept. (Ł)	Municipal Schools (Ł)	Non-municipal Schools (Ł)	School Health Service (Ł)	Total
Recurrent Expenditure	44,341	40,115	804,978	5,734	Ł895,168
Personal Emoluments	14,354	36,438	646,830	2,702	Ł700,324
Salaries	14,354	34,630	646,830	2,603	Ł698,417
Wages	—	1,808	—	99	Ł 1,907
Other	29,987	3,677	158,148	3,032	Ł194,844
General administration	24,591	—	5,540	—	Ł 30,131
Equipment and furniture	874	1,145	46,659	2,475	Ł 51,153
Upkeep and maintenance	—	1,869	13,603	—	Ł 15,472
Transport	2,938	70	—	492	Ł 3,500
Books	—	—	82,487	—	Ł 82,487
Printing and stationery	1,584	593	9,859	65	Ł 12,101
Capital Expenditure	—	9,609	—	—	Ł 9,609
TOTAL	Ł44,341	Ł49,724	Ł804,978	Ł5,734	Ł904,777

a Financial year ending March 31, 1963.
Source: Federal Ministry of Education.

Over-all, federal resources covered over half of all types of expenditure on education in the city--both public and private--and over 90 per cent of capital expenditure. Moreover, federal assistance has been increasing. Between 1963 and 1964 alone, the proportion of total expenditure on education contributed by the federal government increased substantially, reaching the full 70 per cent of elementary school costs.

The Lagos City Council finances the remaining operating costs of municipal and aided nonmunicipal elementary schools. This amounted to a burden on the local tax rates of approximately Ŀ336,000 in 1963-64, as compared with grants received from the federal government of Ŀ704,000.

The federal government meets the net deficits of secondary schools not covered by tuition.

Increases in the federal contribution to education has been accompanied by budgetary attempts to tie expenditure to levels of previous years, but the total costs of education in Lagos have been rapidly growing. This is due both to increases in school-age population of over 10,000 per year and rises in the costs of labor and material. Teachers' salaries have been raised, and these, together with books, constitute 94 per cent of total education costs.

New school construction in the city is provided for in the federal capital budget. In the case of municipal schools, capital improvements are proposed by the chief education officer of the city to the education committee of the city council. Once approved by the council, appropriate funds are included in city budget estimates for approval by the minister of internal affairs. Thereafter, it is up to the minister of education to allocate the funds under its portion of the federal budget.

Similarly, in the Western Region, capital for school improvement and new school construction is provided and authorized by the regional government on advice of the district councils and the local education advisers.

Assessment of School Facilities

Eight years of free elementary school are offered to
all resident pupils in Lagos (including two years of "infant"
classes). The number of children in the appropriate age
brackets in the metropolitan area as a whole is estimated
at approximately 158,000, of which 113,000 are in the city
and 45,000 are in the Western Region portion. In 1963, approximately 143,000 children were attending elementary
school regularly in the area (see Table 6). Over-all, then,
90 per cent of those eligible were enrolled. Breaking the
percentage down by the two sections of the urban area indi-
·cates, however, that 95 per cent of eligible children in the
city and only 80 per cent of those in the Western Region portion are enrolled. The situation is worsening in the regional
portions of the urban complex, for while population growth
is rising faster there, the annual increases in elementary
school enrollment are less than half the comparable increases in the city. (Total increases in enrollment in elementary schools throughout the area are on the order of
10 per cent per year.)

There is a shortage of elementary school classrooms,
for free elementary education was introduced only in 1957.
To accommodate those presently enrolled, schools conduct
two shifts and utilize corridors, courtyards, and sheds as
classroom space. The average number of children per
elementary school class, however, was 38.8 in the city and
35 in the rest of the urban area in 1963, which are within
the local standard calling for a maximum of 40 pupils per
class. Thus, the number of classes, given double shifts, is
not the first and only cause of nonattendance.

Social and economic factors play a large part in the
nonattendance among children of new migrants to the urban
area with extremely low incomes. Costs of books, uniforms,
lunches, and transportation average Ь12 to Ь13 per pupil per
year, which is a deterrent to those families of most uncertain incomes. Health and motivation are additional factors.

In any case, requirements for school construction are
mounting rapidly. If the second shift were eliminated, 1,700
additional new elementary school classrooms would be required to accommodate all presently eligible children in standard class sizes.

TABLE 6

ENROLLMENT IN SCHOOLS BY TYPE

LAGOS URBAN AREA,[a] 1961–63

	1961		1962		1963	
	City	Western Region Portion	City	Western Region Portion	City	Western Region Portion
Elementary	81,780	32,079	98,511	34,571	107,552	35,772
Modern	727	1,914	708	1,990	591	1,945
Secondary grammar	3,980	1,073	6,533	1,201	7,266	1,314
Secondary commercial	2,385	—	2,817	—	3,515	—
Technical institute	1,288	—	1,460	—	1,698	—
Trade & craft center	591	—	538	—	536	—
Teacher training						
Advanced	—	—	145	—	261	—
Grade II	121	208	177	225	194	276
Grade III	354	126	323	100	345	68
Preliminary	88	—	91	—	96	—

[a] Statistics are not available for the Lagos metropolitan area as defined for this study. These figures for the Western Region portion reflect total enrollment in Ikeja Division plus 20 per cent of enrollment in Badagry Division.

Source: Ministry of Education.

The Lagos Executive Development Board has made some estimates of future needs for elementary school classrooms in a report entitled "Planning Standards for the City of Lagos." The report suggests that an elementary school should, at the minimum, occupy four acres of land; that there should be one classroom for each 200 population; and that each classroom should accommodate no more than 40 pupils. Based on these standards the report makes a tentative projection of needs for ten years. This projection calls for 5,000 elementary school classrooms to serve a population of 1 million in the City of Lagos in 1973. The present number of classrooms in the city is 1,696, and taking into consideration double shifts, the present number of classes is 2,775. While the target figure was designed as the requirement for the city itself in 1973, it could also be considered a measure of the present-day requirements for the urban area as a whole, for the area population approximates 1 million. The implication is that elementary school facilities should be doubled.

Shortages in facilities for secondary education are severe. In 1959, out of 3,350 pupils completing elementary education, 1,000 could not be accommodated in secondary education facilities in the city of Lagos. By 1963, the number of elementary school graduates who could not be accommodated in secondary school had risen to more than 5,000. The local estimate of requirements to accommodate at present all eligible students for secondary education is about 150 new classrooms.

According to the standards set forth in the LEDB report, however (one classroom in a secondary school for every 1,000 head of the population, and 30-33 pupils per classroom), the urban area is presently short of accommodations for roughly 15,000 secondary school students, or some 470 classrooms. At present, the central city accounts for nearly three-quarters of the total secondary school enrollment in the whole urban area.

As there is a tuition charge for secondary school, financial factors will continue to limit enrollment for some time into the future. The average secondary school pupil in the city of Lagos pays in excess of Ł65 per year for tuition and fees alone, and a total of about Ł130 per year including expenses. Tuition and fees in the secondary schools

in the Western Region, as suggested by a special regional
study commission, range from approximately Ł38 to Ł50 per
year, not including expenses. A limited number of federal
and regional scholarships are available and there are a few
scholarships offered by voluntary agencies and commercial
firms.

Shortage of trained and qualified teachers is a serious
problem throughout Nigeria and, while the situation is less
severe within the Lagos urban area than in the rural sections
of the country, it is nevertheless of concern. The pupil-
teacher ratio in the primary schools in the metropolis was
approximately 32:1 in 1963. This same ratio in the secondary
schools was about 33:1. Many of the teachers in the elementary schools, however, are not recipients of teaching
certificates. Certified teachers are those who have earned a
professional diploma of one of several grades. Some of
the uncertified teachers have no professional training, while
others have not passed the final examinations for a certificate. Many of these are graduates of elementary or modern
schools without secondary education.

The lowest level of certification is "grade three, "
awarded to those who have completed the two-year course at
a grade-three teacher-training college. To have been ad-
mitted to the teacher-training college, candidates must be
graduates of a modern school course or have taught for two
years after leaving elementary school. "Grade-two" teachers
include graduates of elementary schools with at least two
years' teaching experience who have then completed a four-
year course of study at a grade-two teacher-training college.
Above grade two are holders of certificates from the Institute
of Education at the University of Ibadan, or certificates of
the United Kingdom Ministry of Education. (These are grade-
two teachers with at least four years' further teaching experience and one year of course work at Ibadan or London.) The
small group at the top of the ladder are the "grade-one"
teachers, who have passed the examinations for the general
certificate of education at the advanced level in two or three
subjects and have had an additional four years of postgraduate
teaching experience.

Secondary school teachers are similarly graded. The
bulk of them are untrained graduates of secondary schools or

graduates of grade-two teacher-training colleges. The top levels include teachers who have received a B. A. from universities or professional postgraduate degrees.

While this complex system of teacher certification is based upon prescribed courses and examinations, the only condition for actually teaching is that the person be registered as a qualified teacher with the government education authorities. Temporary registration is permitted frequently, particularly in areas where new schools are being created. According to the Ministry of Education, slightly under one-third of the teachers in the elementary schools in Lagos are not certified, and most of these have no secondary education. This is a considerable improvement over the situation in 1956, however, when over 50 per cent of the elementary school teachers in Lagos were uncertified. And almost all the teachers in the few government-owned schools do hold teaching certificates of grade two or grade three.

Intergovernmental Relationships

In summary, most primary schools in the metropolitan area are financed by the federal or regional government, managed by voluntary agencies, regulated by the federal or regional government, and aided and supervised by local authorities. Most secondary schools are owned and managed by voluntary agencies, but subsidized, regulated, and supervised by the federal or regional government. Local authorities act as agents of higher government for carrying out some educational policies. In addition, as education is a concurrent subject, the federal government has extended assistance and grants to the regions for the development of secondary institutions, as well as university education.

Occasional meetings are held between the regional permanent secretary for education and the federal permanent secretary for education, but there has been no coordinated educational planning by the two governments with respect to the urban area.

Planning for secondary and elementary education is the primary responsibility of the regions throughout the country. In one aspect of educational planning, however, the federal government has played an important role. In connection with its concern with the larger problems of economic growth

and of underemployment, the federal government established
the National Manpower Board in 1962. This board is charged
with determining Nigeria's long-range manpower needs, and
formulating for the National Economic Council programs for
manpower development through university expansion and secondary school training. It attempts to coordinate the manpower training policies and activities of the federal and regional ministries. The regional governments participate in
the manpower board. Joint educational planning has been
limited to this field. The board is mainly interested in high-
level manpower; that is, university graduates, professional
personnel, and technicians. The federal government assists
the regions' efforts to develop technical education on a modest scale and has, with foreign assistance, undertaken some
policy studies for this purpose.[3] The Federal Science Center
at Lagos was established to train science teachers for the
elementary and secondary schools throughout the country.
In addition, the National Advance Teacher Training College
recruits students from the whole nation and thereby influ-
ences elementary and secondary institutions outside the federal territory.

In the absence of urban education planning, certain
problems persist in Lagos, however. School facilities in
the Western Region portion of the metropolitan area are
poor compared to those within the city. Education has not
played an ameliorative role with respect to the relatively
high crime and disorganized social patterns in the new,
dense sections of the urban complex that consist mainly of
uprooted migrant populations. Under the present government
structure, there is little stimulus for coordinated social
planning in relation to urban education. The local-government authorities are responsible to different electorates as
well as to different supervising governments. General educational planning by the Western Region does not deal with
particular problems of the Lagos urban area such as crime,
unsanitary living conditions for the children, and very fast-
growing needs for technical and vocational education in conjunction with new industrial estates.

In addition, some problems result from the diffusion
of managerial responsibility among government agencies and
manifold voluntary agencies. The education plant existing in
Nigeria at the time of independence in 1960 was almost entirely private. Therefore, the decision taken by the

government to establish a public education system first by
regulating and financing the existing private institutions was
a valid and necessary one. *

At the same time, the integration of the private
schools into the public education system makes it difficult to
apply uniform standards and to rationalize educational development (for example, to have different types of schools in a
proportion suitable to educational needs). ** The voluntary
agencies pressure the Ministry of Education and the Lagos
City Council to support schools that are under their operation,
and they oppose changes in their programs. As the agencies
depend upon public financing, however, the governments do
have a base of power that they could utilize for greater control over the schools, while they continue to develop new
government schools on the basis of planning assessments
of social and economic needs.

Educational development in Lagos should be related
to problems of structural unemployment. There is a severe
shortage of skilled artisans and technicians, below the level
considered by the manpower board, and an excess of general
primary school graduates in the labor force. These "school
leavers" comprise a large portion of new urban migrants.

---

* For example, in Calcutta, where the same situation existed,
state and local government are not aiding or effectively regulating private institutions that charge high tuition, but rather
are attempting to establish separate free public primary
schools. It has proved impossible to establish free public
primary schools at a rate that would accommodate in a short
period a large proportion of the eligible pupils. In the meantime, private schools are not meeting the priority needs of
the area and local governments are incapable of carrying out
their legal responsibility to provide universal education.

** Secondary grammar schools have multiplied in parts of
the urban area while technical schools are in very short
supply. In 1961, there were 1,200 eligible applicants for
180 places at the Yaba Trade Center.

Unemployment is high among them, but to return to their village and farming or to accept menial work is considered a
humiliation.   Thus, education aimed at employment problems
must both provide skills and modify attitudes toward work.
Although the federal government is committed to expanding
technical and vocational education at the secondary level,
the National Development Plan does not identify operational
targets and programs in this category, which represents
a serious public policy gap. [4] Even within the federal government, this subject lies somewhere between the Ministry
of Labor and the Ministry of Education.   And for the urban
area as a whole, it falls through the cracks between the
federal government, and the Western Region and the operating voluntary agencies.

NOTES TO CHAPTER 5

1. Otto Koenigsberger, et al. , Metropolitan Lagos
(New York: U. N. Commissioner for Technical Assistance,
1964).

2. See Peter Marris, Family and Social Change in an
African City (London: Routledge and Kegan Paul, 1961).
Marris conducted a survey of central Lagos in which he
found that nine-tenths of the resident owners had been born
in Lagos and maintained modified traditional social practices. For example, 61 per cent regularly attended meetings of their kinship group, which was both a business and
a welfare unit. Some 87 per cent of the women in central
Lagos were employed in retail trading for which their
location was essential. Within the family compounds,
crafts and selling were engaged in by women while they
were caring for the children.

3. Recommendations for a National Plan of Vocational
and Technical Education in the Republic of Nigeria (Lagos:
Ford Foundation, 1966).

4. A recent attempt to bridge this gap is represented
by the Report of the Comparative Technical Education Semi-
nar Abroad and Recommendations for a National Plan of
Vocational and Technical Education in the Republic of
Nigeria (Lagos: Ford Foundation, 1966).

CHAPTER **6** COMPARATIVE TRENDS
AND PROBLEMS IN
URBAN ADMINISTRATION

The participants in urban government in Lagos are
local, state, and national authorities, who do not have distinct jurisdiction over clusters of public activity, but inter-
penetrating responsibilities. Local authorities in metropolitan Lagos derived their powers from specific statutory and
administrative delegation from national or regional government. The duties delegated to them are primarily manage-
rial--to operate established facilities and public services,
such as public health clinics, schools, and conservancy services. In large part, legal regulation, program formulation,
and financial decisions are outputs of higher authorities.
The developmental role of local governments has therefore
been limited while their caretaker duties have expanded.

The involvement of several levels of government in
any one urban public service is a common trend in urban administration generally. Thus, we do not find education, for
example, the exclusive responsibility of national government
and water supply that of local government in any urban area,
but rather we discover that both governments are involved in
each service with distinctions between them more according
to particular roles they perform in producing the service
(proposing projects, planning, constructing, financing, managing, approving, regulating, etc.), rather than according to
public purposes. The distribution of roles varies considerably in terms of the degree of centralization of the governmental system, but the minimal common role of national or
state governments is authorization of capital funds available
for urban projects, and the minimal common role of local
authorities is management of routine services. Lagos falls
toward the centralized end of the spectrum.

This pattern of administration generally renders
various levels of government interdependent for program

achievement. State or national authorities depend on local governments to implement many programs and to bring problems and suggestions to their attention. On the other hand, local authorities find themselves dependent on grants, loans, and approvals from higher authorities when they seek to extend, create, or improve public facilities. Intense intergovernmental communication and willingness to cooperate are prerequisites to reasonably expeditious administrative processes under these conditions.

An intergovernmental partnership approach to urban administration depends in large part upon the attitudes of the officials involved. The tendency in Lagos for higher officials to view local authorities as subjects to be controlled and restrained on the one hand, or competitors to be politically mollified on the other, is not consistent with such an approach--but neither is the tendency of local officials to view higher government as an interfering nuisance to be held at arm's length whenever possible. Political party cleavage between the city and national government has reinforced both these tendencies. The most obvious results of a lack of consensus and constructive communication between the two levels of government are stalemate and congested administration, witnessed by delays in budget approvals and tax collection, in pupil enrollment, in sewer extensions, etc. Certain legal and organizational arrangements (such as intergovernmental planning efforts and policy committees, streamlined approval procedures, and/or vesting responsibility for liaison and supervision in a single higher government officer with specific city or metropolitan jurisdiction) may enhance opportunities for smooth cooperative relationships, but underlying patterns of political power and personal attitudes appear to be crucial determinants of their effect.

In any case, there are few pressures to shift significant powers for urban development and urban administration from national or regional authorities to local government in metropolitan Lagos. There appears to be little popular commitment to or identification with urban local councils. (This observation does not apply generally to the rest of the nation, however.) Various ethnic and interest groups tend to express their demands to national and regional authorities, particularly within the city, where the federal ministries have headquarters. Most citizen responses to government have been generalized public protests, which have had similar degrees of success against both local and national authorities (e. g. , those regarding enforcement of traffic laws and slum clearance). Moreover, the expansion rates of public services provided directly by federal agencies (water supply, for example) compare favorably with those of local services.

There are significant pressures, on the other hand, tending toward continued centralization. National and regional control over allocating scarce public capital funds is inherent in the concept of planned development. Moreover, dependence on foreign aid channeled through national authorities for all major proposed urban improvements reinforces this control. Thus, for example, while the Lagos City Council is formally responsible for transit and sewage services, proposed projects in both categories would be undertaken by foreign assistants working with national authorities. The staff resources of local authorities have been extremely limited, and current inquiries into the city government are not likely to increase confidence in local government. Thus, delegation of further implementing duties, as for example those relating to water supply or secondary education, are unlikely in the near future. Above all, the centrifugal tendencies in Nigeria as a whole and concomitant political instability dampen the enthusiasm of regional or national governments for sharing powers within their domains. These factors limit the competence of local authorities, which even now have greater legal responsibility than they exercise. The corollary, of course, is that if the national government does not accept its responsibility to carry out urban improvements and assume the necessary financial burdens, the improvements will not be made. Evidence from other centralized systems suggests that continual pressure from officials or constituencies within the metropolitan area are key factors in stimulating such response from national or state authorities.

This study is one among several similar case studies of government and administration. * Among the nations in

---

* The other case studies analyzed to date are of Calcutta, India; Casablanca, Morocco; Davao, Philippines; Karachi, Pakistan; Lima, Peru; Lodz, Poland; Paris, France; Stockholm, Sweden; Toronto, Canada; Valencia, Venezuela; and

which we worked, Nigeria ranks low (of high, medium, and low) in gross national product per capita and its rate of increase, literacy, and percentage of population in cities over 20,000 population. It is the newest independent nation in the group and one of the least advanced technologically and economically.

One of the major observations emerging from comparative analysis, however, is that the nature of explosive demands for governmental services arising from rapid urbanization and their fundamental implications for administration are similar in very different areas. The severity of urban problems and the intensity of certain administrative problems differs, but the uniformity in the nature of the problems is remarkable.

Deficiencies of public service output in fields of housing, transportation, water supply, sewage, schools, and hospitals are great in Lagos because, in addition to governmental output's not keeping up with population growth in the last decade (which is a near universal urban condition), the public service base was rudimentary and in some categories (e. g. , public schools) nonexistent to start with. Because of their severity in Lagos, these deficiencies not only limit the convenience of urban life and economic growth potential, but also threaten basic health of the urban citizens.

Under conditions of rapid urban growth, the first common essential attribute of effective government is a capacity for innovation: new investment, new problem solutions, new developmental activities. A government system characterized by a caretaker stance does not respond to the population growth and socio-economic changes that urbanization signifies. Government activity and expenditure lag behind these changes in all urban areas we have studied.

Zagreb, Yugoslavia. With the exception of the Karachi study, which was designed and carried out by Professor Herbert Kagi, these were undertaken by the Institute of Public Administration according to a uniform research outline.

There are several factors identifiable from our case
studies as stimulants or prerequisites for continuing innovation in urban administration. Systematic perception of
needs and demands for their fulfillment by groups influential
in or on government are among these prerequisites. It is
the exception to find citizen groups and political parties that
consistently express demands for urban public services. In
Lagos, while the conditions of urban life are directly felt by
the citizens, they do not consistently expect government to
alter these conditions. One of the authors witnessed a monumental rush hour traffic jam in Lagos caused by a minor ac-
cident. Hundreds of halted travelers gathered to debate the
cause and complain of traffic conditions, but an hour passed
before anyone decided that the "authorities" might be called
to clear up the mess. The expectations for government action are higher in the more developed areas studied, but
they still fall far short of felt needs. *

In most of the urban areas we examined, problem
identification, program proposals, and innovative pressures
are more frequently generated by governmental or bureau-
cratic groups; party and popular groups tend to be reactive.
This phenomenon is marked in Lagos. Citizen groups
there protest, by march or demonstration, actions taken or
proposed to be taken. Each group thereby exercises crucial
power on the one issue it chooses, but there is little demand
for general improvements. The demands for workers' housing generated by the trade union strike in 1964 is a notable
exception, and it did elicit response from the national government.

The political parties involved in local elections in
metropolitan Lagos compete in terms of national, not urban,
issues. This has been the case in all of the urban areas
studied where the party structure reflects ideological or
broad social cleavages. Even in Toronto, where candidates
for local office do not run on party tickets, local elections
have not revolved primarily around substantive urban policy
issues.

----

* No original attitude surveys were undertaken. The observations are based on the authors' experience, and conclusions
drawn from examination of the press, election campaigns, and
interest group action.

Thus, leadership within the government and bureaucracy is a factor crucial to innovation and development in urban administration in most areas. The general lack of leadership devoted to defining urban problems of Lagos and to engineering consensus and action on them is its most serious problem. While public appointments and contracts are highly politicized, policies are not. Moreover, the vested interests among government officials in the status quo are intense. Officials with an interest in conservancy contracts oppose progress on a sewer system. Officials with interests in bus purchase contracts oppose alternative approaches to transit improvements.

In part, effective leadership for urban government is an extraorganizational phenomenon. It has risen and fallen over time in single areas with no accompanying changes in government structure. But comparison of the twelve case areas leads one to the proposition that certain structural factors tend to facilitate its development. One is the existence of continuing planning efforts that are closely linked to the key decision-makers and that systematically define urban service goals and formulate operational program proposals that may form a basis for consensus and coordinated action, or at least a basis for policy conflict that may be ultimately resolved. This type of planning has not occurred in Lagos. The one-time proposals of the foreign-assistance planners have not entered into the political or administrative mainstreams for the most part.

Experience in Lagos raises interesting questions as to the limitations of foreign assistance on matters of governmental organization and general policy formulation. The formal and explicit terms of their assignments exclude overt consideration of political issues by foreign or ieternational missions. This, however, results in a significant paradox, for any proposals they may make dealing with public policy or government structure have political ramifications: They increase the advantages and disadvantages of various groups in government and the bureaucracy. Moreover, events in Lagos demonstrate that the roots of many of its administrative problems are political. In consequence, advice that is not at least tacitly based on assessment of political problems and feasibility and is responsive to the political imperatives of the existing government is not likely to be followed, in the first place, and even if followed is not likely to produce the results foreseen, in the second. In general, our comparative studies confirm that any body of administrative principles must be framed in terms of appropriate political variables in order to have general international validity.

In general, our case studies reveal some common themes in foreign-assistance advice on metropolitan problems. One is an emphasis on using public corporations rather than general government agencies for public service development. Experience in the areas studied suggests that the advantages and disadvantages of this form of institution deserve careful examination. Lagos, for example, demonstrates that there is no magic improvement automatically arising from the corporate form. Personnel problems, corruption, and un-economic pricing have occurred within public corporations and development authorities as well as in general government. These underlying problems are the crucial variables in improvement. Another common recommendation is for consolidated metropolitan government, which is discussed later in this chapter.

Returning to the factors that tend to facilitate the development of leadership, concentrated executive responsibility appears to qualify. On the local level in Lagos, the direct control of bureaucracy by the council (and its individual members), without intervening executive organs, facilitates the injection of private interests of the councilmen into administrative action and fragments formal power that might become the basis of innovative leadership. On the national and regional levels, key decision-making powers with respect to metropolitan Lagos are dispersed among various ministries and statutory corporations, all of which have nation-wide or region-wide interest and therefore do not tend to assume responsibility for leadership in Lagos. Even the Ministry of Lagos Affairs had little policy responsibility for many aspects of development in the city. Legally defined responsibility backed by administrative capability to cope with specifically local or metropolitan concerns is an important foundation of leadership in urban government.

In general, the most conspicuous lags in problem definition and program formulation among the areas we examined occurred where there are weak local authorities and no metropolitan institutions. Weak metropolitan institutions, which have little influence on higher authorities who retain effective powers do not appear to alter this situation radically, as was witnessed in Lodz, Casablanca, Valencia, and Davao. A metropolitan institution that is wholly controlled by higher government (it may even be a field agency of higher government) in nations with centralized decision-making power may have far more influence and impact than a weak but separate metropolitan tier. Its planning and policy formulation activities can also have considerable effect without its absorbing essential operating responsibilities if it is responsive to the executive centers of power and if those powers are concentrated.

This brings us to a second key attribute of effective government in vast urban complexes: a network of constructive metropolitan relationships to deal with geographically extensive issues. The existence of these relationships is of first importance; the degree to which they are being institutionalized, however, is increasing generally in most of the urban areas examined. In Lagos, constructive relationships are themselves lacking, and therefore creation of metropolitan institutions alone is not likely to effect significant coordination.

Influential metropolitan institutions that engage in development planning and attempt to correlate public programs do sustain continuous monitoring of interrelated problems and proposals at minimum. Comparison of our case studies does not support an unequivocal assertion, however, that all-purpose metropolitan government is essential to effective urban administration. In the first place, metropolitan governments are only as effective as their internal capabilities permit. Underlying personnel and fiscal problems are not mitigated by metropolitan organization, per se, but are often replicated in metropolitan tiers.

Second, many of the specific problems created by structural fragmentation in Lagos can be mitigated by mechanisms other than metropolitan government. Specific intergovernmental agreements and cooperative efforts generally take care of problems of operating program conflict where there is general commitment on the part of officials to expediting action on urban problems. The LEDB could be authorized to acquire land in the Western Region for construction purposes, just as the Paris housing agency operates outside the city limits. The relative service deficiencies

in the Western Region portion of the metropolitan area could
be reduced by increased regional investment, possibly with
aid of federal grants, and local tax equalization procedures.
The Western Region could consolidate the district councils
in the metropolitan area and establish a strong urban government counterpart to the city government.

Third, if interrelated development projects are co-
herent in conception and design, there is little evidence that
program achievement is greater if they are all executed by
the same agency. This applies not only to aspects of geo-
graphical coordination but also to aspects of interservice
coordination. For example, if programs for water supply
extensions and a sewage system for metropolitan Lagos each
took into consideration the implications of the other, there is
little obvious payoff from having them executed by one metropolitan agency. Similarly, there is certainly room for
land development activities by two housing agencies in the
metropolitan area if their plans are consistent in terms of
job and home locations and transportation linkages.

A conclusion that does emerge clearly from the study
of Lagos as well as those of the other case areas, however,
is that there are several advantages to metropolitan-scale
action of several types, particularly planning and development program review, establishment of transit systems, and
functions that use scarce regional resources, such as potable
water supply in Lagos or public borrowing. A multipurpose
tier to engage in these functions or at least to coordinate
authorities doing so raises fewer practical problems of interservice conflict than does the proliferation of autonomous
single-purpose metropolitan authorities alone. Many areas
have followed the second course first and subsequently have
attempted to devise mechanisms for interrelating metropolitan agencies, be they autonomous authorities, national government field services, or intermunicipal special districts.

The dimensions of metropolitan coordination, and
therefore appropriate mechanisms for institutionalizing it,
differ from area to area with the distribution of decision-
making powers. In Lagos, these powers are predominantly
vested in national and regional governments. If the lessons
of other areas can be applied, metropolitan institutions (such
as a greater Lagos council) that do not bring these two units
into relationship with each other will have limited impact on

policy coherence. A Greater Lagos Council could formulate metropolitan policies and urge these policies on the higher authorities. Its success in this respect, however, would depend on reversal of the downward flow of initiative, such as it is, in government for Lagos, which would require political support, particularly in light of the importance of foreign assistance. A more direct approach to coordination in a centralized system is made by mechanisms that link the relevant federal and state agencies for purposes of concerted action in the metropolitan area. This is the course being pursued in Paris and Calcutta, for example, where emerging metropolitan institutions are mainly national and state agencies.

In any case, the establishment of constructive metropolitan relationships in Lagos is contingent upon political developments. The conflict between the Western Region and advocates of extension of the federal territory boundaries is intensified by the current demands of the Nigerian regions for greater autonomy and by communal strife within the nation. The intensity of the conflict and the fact that it penetrates into most issues of urban administration are fundamental obstacles to pragmatic cooperation and joint planning, which have proved fairly effective in other urban areas of the world that are dissected by higher government boundaries. There are real conflicts of interest among different segments of most urban areas of the world. Even where metropolitan or higher units of government have formal powers to impose solutions, this is seldom feasible if the conflicts are intensive and reinforced by party, economic, or ethnic cleavages. On the other hand, where the parties are willing to compromise for practical purposes, solutions are frequently arrived at without coercion or major reorganization, although the latter two phenomenon are increasingly being resorted to in large metropolitan areas.

It is essential to substantial improvement in urban life that political conflict in Lagos be contained at least for purposes of major development projects. Given the present distribution of population and employment, it will make little sense to create sewage and transit systems that stop abruptly at the city line. And emerging social problems in the dense near-in suburbs most certainly will spill into the city.

A third key attribute of urban government is expanding staff resources, particularly skills relating to new technical

services (from sewage systems to poverty programs) and
large-scale management. While public administration in
older, more advanced areas has found it difficult to compete
with the productive sector for human skills, in Lagos and
the other areas with comparably low economic and educational development, the scarcity of skills is a general condition of the society. As the economic functions of government
expand in response to urbanization, not only the number of
public personnel required expands but also the required educational and experiential qualifications for them expand.
The transition, for example, from night-soil collection to
construction and operation of a closed sewage system in
Lagos, or that from operation of a bus company to establishment of a rapid transit system, involve a net shift from
laboring employees to technicians and managers in the personnel profile of urban government. Rapid Nigerianization
of the civil service, dwindling number of expatriate officers,
and the necessarily slow process of educational development,
however, are short-run obstacles to effecting this shift
efficiently. * In addition to technicians--such as engineers,
hydrologists, and architects--middle-level supervisory and
management personnel are in seriously short supply within
local government in Lagos, as well as in Calcutta and other
developing areas. The problem extends as well to private
contractors who perform works for the city. This has direct
effects on program achievement and maintenance of public
plants, because employees with low educational levels are
only loosely supervised.

There is little doubt that personnel training and education, to develop both specific skills and generally practical
attitudes, is of high priority for improvement of urban administration in developing areas such as Lagos. Where the
human resources required are generally scarce, as in Nigeria, an approach to personnel recruitment problems that
aims merely to raise salaries and increase attractiveness of
the posts without attempting to increase the number of potential candidates may do little except enrich the civil servants.

---

* According to the Federal Public Service Commission, the
percentages of senior posts in the federal civil service held by
Nigerians grew from 48 in 1958 to 87 in 1963.

There may be advantages to metropolitanization of local government in this respect, if it is carried out in such a
way as to consolidate staff resources. Thus, for example,
there are two tiers of government in Casablanca--the muni-
cipalities and the metropolitan prefecture--but the administrative agencies of both are consolidated at the prefecture
level (as have been the agencies of the city of Paris and
Department of Seine.) On the other hand, the two-tier systems in Toronto and Zagreb (where personnel shortages are
milder problems) do involve some duplication of staff needs.
Davao and Valencia have single-tier metropolitan governments. In the latter, however, local staff is rudimentary
and all major urban services are directly provided by national or state authorities.

The personnel problems of local government in metropolitan Lagos including shortages, incompetence, and
corruption, have been found within national and regional government and public corporations as well. This situation underscores a significant observation of our comparative study:
analysis in some depth is required to derive the practical implications of obvious administrative problems. It is widely
recognized that the personnel weaknesses of local authorities
are significant brakes on delegation of powers to them. A
common response to these weaknesses is retention of centralized powers in urban administration or delegation of powers to "businesslike" development corporations. Another
response is centralization of personnel administration itself,
as by the unified local personnel system in the Western Region. If, however, patterns of incompetence or corruption
are replicated in higher government and public corporations,
those responses will shift power from one group to another
but will not alter the basic administrative patterns. Significant change in administrative behavior is contingent upon
treating the ailment, not its symptoms. In any case, technical assistance to local authorities and enhancement of their
internal capabilities should precede delegation of powers to
them. Otherwise, delegation leads to disillusionment and
recentralization with no discernible administrative improvements.

Because of the upheavals represented by current official inquiries into local government in Lagos and Nigerian
public corporations, the problem of corruption deserves additional comment. Some writers have associated what we

here call corruption--or illegal diversion of public benefits to
private interests--with developing societies, specifically with
their particularist and diffused cultural orientations and
norms. Others have pointed out that bribery as a method of
allocating scarce resources is not without pragmatic usefulness. Our comparative analysis yields some insights on
both of these points.

First, corruption in public service does not seem to
vary from nation to nation with level of economic development.
Urban political systems in highly industrialized settings have
been plagued with these problems, and at least segments of
the civil service in several developing areas have shown high
incidence of honesty and integrity. Effective legal checks together with a prestigious ethos in civil service corps are
associated with the absence of these problems in most cases.
Some societies as a whole can be found that appear to be
remarkably law abiding. Sweden, in our sample, qualifies,
and there seems to be little incidence of irregularity in the
public service or political circles in Stockholm. But such
cultural attitudes do not appear to relate directly to economic
development. The United States compares unfavorably with
Sweden in this respect. And in France and Lodz, for example, strong legal checks are relied upon heavily to prevent corruption.

As to the second point, practical reasons for con-
demning corruption, as here defined, can be identified in
Lagos without reference to any exclusively moral values, if
we accept the official values of the government itself, which
call for maximum development with scarce resources. There
is waste in these terms, for example, when buses unsuitable
for Lagos streets are purchased and transit fares are not
channeled into public revenues. There is waste when incom-
petent contractors are engaged to utilize scarce capital funds.
And there is a built-in bias against improvement of urban
life when political leaders have a vested interest in high rents
and outmoded services. Finally, public cynicism toward
government reinforces resistance to law enforcement and tax
collection.

Closely linked to the qualifications and behavior of
administrative staffs in urban government generally is their
relationship with political officials. In Lagos, as well as in

Calcutta and Lima, where elected councils dominate executive functions, detailed political interference in administrative action is common and there is little flow of policy advice from the administrative officers to the political officials. Trends in other areas signify, however, that with the rising complexity of urban administration, this flow of advice is vital to sound decision-making, and delegation of day-to-day managerial decisions to the bureaucracy is essential in order both to free officials for policy concerns and to keep the administrative processes moving at a reasonable pace. Again, we find underlying political factors affecting administrative problems, for intense politicization of contracts, appointments, and purchases gives the councilmen in Lagos little taste for delegation.

Increased delegation to the bureaucracy requires as a counterbalance, intensified general controls over policy directions on the part of political officials. An attempt is being made in many areas to strengthen such control by use of permanent boards appointed by councils, strong chief executives, or professional chief administrative officers subordinate to political organs. One is led to conclude that the structure of local government in Lagos heightens the council's power over distribution of monetary benefits, but renders it incapable of playing an important role in formulating general policies and development projects for the city.

A fourth attribute of urban government essential to response to urban problems is, of course, expansion of public finance. Local revenues generally do not expand at a rate commensurate with population growth and urban needs. Lagos is a statistical exception to this generalization only because the base of local-government expenditure a decade ago was negligible. All expansion of local revenues in Lagos is contingent upon higher government approval, for the tax rates are geared annually to budget estimates. As in most areas, there is small leeway for local expansion of resources without higher government action. In Lagos, this leeway consists mainly in the potential for increasing collection efficiency.

In addition, popular local opposition to rises in fees for public services (e. g. , water and transit charges) has been felt in widely differing types of urban areas throughout the world, but generally seems to take far less toll of elected officials after raises are effected than most politicians expect. Certainly raises in water rates in Lagos that allowed distribution to families now buying from their neighbors should make some friends as well as enemies, if accompanied by real systems improvements and some public relations efforts.

By comparison to the range of areas studied, Lagos is poor, of course. But there is little evidence that all reasonable sources are being tapped. There is wealth in the city which is taxed over-all at far lower rates than other areas. Policy decisions by higher government, in fact, put a lower ceiling on revenues for urban administration than do economic factors.

The most important functions of government for Lagos in the next decade, however, is investment in urban infrastructure. This was illustrated in examination of each of the four public services reviewed. There is little doubt that economic factors--low rate of savings, weak credit market, and priorities for productive investment--are crucial brakes on capital investment, which with very few exceptions cannot be adequately financed out of current revenues. National and regional control of capital funds for urban and other investments implies their continuing importance in urban government. This is a common dimension of intergovernmental relationships in urban administration in most nations of the world. As the capital of Nigeria, Lagos is in a good competitive position to claim a share of what funds are allocated by the federal government to public infrastructure (which is not universally the case with capital cities, some of which are disadvantaged by explicit policy of national authorities). The tendency of the federal government to date, however, has been to assign priority to investments in showcase projects (slum clearance, a skyscraper, and hotels, for example) and industry, rather than to public services.

Because of the generally important role of higher governments in urban administration, another key attribute of governmental systems for urban areas is intensive and constructive relationships between local and higher authorities. The problems adhering to these relationships in Lagos that were noted at the beginning of this chapter are common. In most areas in which local-national relationships for urban development are relatively smooth and free of stalemate, intergovernmental exchange of information and views, including negotiation before budgets, programs, and aid applications are formally made, occurs frequently. Coincidence of political party control of the different units also contributes to cooperative attitudes where urban projects are politicized.

In addition to informal relationships, the exercise of formal administrative controls over local authorities is a source of problems. They are seldom exercised for purposes of producing cohesive approaches to urban problems, but are aimed at assuring legality, regularity, and protection of national government interests. Detailed and overlapping administrative reviews and approvals frequently do not produce effective net control for these purposes. We have observed from the case studies that there are at least three common attributes of effective control, all of which are missing in Lagos. The first is that the supervising authorities be given stable assignments, not subject to frequent political transfer, and that they be personally committed to insuring legality and aiding local authorities. The second is that there be a few key controlling powers, not watered down by so many approval duties that the reviewing officer can only give perfunctory attention to each. The strongest of these are fiscal controls, including both pre-audit and post-audit. The growth of local-government activities makes pre-audit nearly impossible to administer efficiently unless carried out by an officer on the spot. Both Zagreb and Paris offer effective examples of it, however. In French local authorities, as well as in national ministries, an officer of the Ministry of Finance is posted as treasurer. He executes fiscal transactions authorized by the appropriate executive officer and applies legal criteria in doing so. The fiscal transactions of public institutions in Yugoslavia, including those of local authorities, must be executed through the branches of the national bank, where they are subject to continuing checks by the social accounting service.

The third attribute of effective control in many areas is the codification of criteria for supervision in a body of law and administrative regulations. Administrative law may spell out, for example, procedures of public bidding for local contracts, required contract forms and specifications, and substantive aspects of permissible contract arrangements. This codification produces stable and predetermined criteria for both local authorities and reviewing officers, reduces the

need for prior approval of each act, and may provide for
court review.

Events in Lagos and several other developing areas
manifest a cycle consisting of detailed but ineffective administrative controls, crisis points in local administration,
suspension or reorganization of local authorities, and
reemergence of previous problems. In Lagos, 1966-67 is a
crisis year, as was 1953-54. The local council is under
suspension, and public inquiries are revealing that undesirable patterns of behavior have thrived in the city's administration.

Our studies suggest that there are key points in the
political and administrative structure where change might
be concentrated to break out of problem cycles—particularly
aspects of executive leadership, metropolitan cooperation,
legal control, and personnel development.

Nigeria is fighting for its life as a nation against
strong centrifugal political and social forces. Most of the
problems of metropolitan Lagos are microcosms of national
political and administrative problems. Solutions for Lagos
that might better equip it with a governmental system capable
of achieving maximum improvements in urban life and economy within available resources are first and foremost contingent upon the outcome of national upheavals and reorganization.

SELECTED BIBLIOGRAPHY

SELECTED BIBLIOGRAPHY

Official Documents and Reports

Imrie, Sir John. Report Into the Relationships Between the Federal Government and the Lagos Town Council. Lagos: Federal Government Printer, 1959.

Jones, G. C., and Lucas, B. Keith. Report on the Administration of the Lagos Town Council. Lagos: Lagos Town Council, 1963.

Koenigsberger, Otto; Abrams, Charles; Kobe, Susumu; Shapiro, Maurice; and Wheeler, Michael. Metropolitan Lagos. (Prepared for the Government of Nigeria.) New York: United Nations Commissioner for Technical Assistance (65-34179), 1964. (Mimeo.)

Lagos City Council. Accounts for the Year Ended 31st March 1962. Lagos: 1962

_____. Accounts for the Year Ended 31st March 1963. Lagos: 1963.

_____. Annual Report. Lagos: 1959-60; 1960-61; 1961-62; 1962-63; and 1963-64.

_____. Estimates. Lagos: 1962-63; 1964-65; 1965-66.

_____. Lagos Municipal Transport Service Estimates. Lagos: 1964-65 and 1965-66.

_____. Memorandum Submitted to the Commissioner of Inquiry (Saville) Into the Administration of the Lagos City Council. Lagos: Town Clerk, 1966.

Lagos Executive Development Board. Annual Report and Accounts. Lagos: 1956-57; 1957-58; 1958-59; 1959-60; 1960-61; 1961-62; 1962-63.

177

Lagos Executive Development Board. Board News. (Quarterly Journal.) Lagos: 1964, 1965.

Nigeria, Federal Government of. Annual Reports of the Ministry of Labour and Social Welfare Division. Lagos: Government Printers, 1960, 1961.

_____. Annual Report of the Public Works Department, 1958-1959. Lagos: Government Printers, 1960.

_____. Federal Census Office Reports. Lagos: Government Printers, 1964.

_____. First Annual Report on the Revolving Loans Fund for Industry Up to 31st March, 1961. Lagos: Government Printers, 1962.

_____. The Laws of the Federation of Nigeria and Lagos. Lagos: Government Printers, 1959. Chapters 56, 97, 98, 99.

_____. National Development Plan, 1962-1968. Lagos: Federal Ministry of Economic Development, 1962.

_____. National Development Plan Progress Report. Lagos: Government Printers, 1964.

_____. Proceedings of the Commission of Inquiry into the Administration of the Lagos City Council (Saville Commission). Lagos: Federal Government, 1966.

_____. Proposals for the Constitution of the Federal Republic of Nigeria. Lagos: Government Printers, 1963.

_____. Report of the Commission on the Review of Wages, Salary and Conditions of Service of the Junior Employees of the Governments of the Federation and in Private Establishments, 1963-1964. Lagos: Government Printers, 1964.

_____. Report on Education Development in Lagos. Lagos: Government Printers, 1957.

_____. Report on the Nigeria Federal Elections. Lagos: Government Printers, 1959.

Nigeria, Federal Government of. A Report of the Registra-
    tion of Title to Land in Lagos. Lagos: Federal Gov-
    ernment Printer, 1957.

Nigeria, Federal Ministry of Education. Annual Digest of
    Education Statistics. Lagos: Government Printers,
    1961 and 1962.

_____. Statistics of Education in Nigeria. Lagos: Gov-
    ernment Printers, 1963.

Nigeria, National Manpower Board. Manpower Situation in
    Nigeria. Lagos: Government Printers, 1963.

Nigeria, National Manpower, Federation. A Study of Ni-
    geria's Professional Manpower in Selected Occupations.
    Lagos: Government Printers, 1964.

Northern Nigeria Government. Local Government Year Book.
    Zaria: Institute of Administration, 1963.

Rapson, R. N. Report of an Inquiry Into Alleged Irregularities
    by the Lagos Town Council in Connection with the Col-
    lection of Money and the Allocation of Market Stalls in
    Respect of Proposed Ereko and Oko-Awo. Lagos:
    Federal Government Printer, 1959.

Simpson, S. R. Report of a Working Party on Registration
    of Ownership of Land, in Lagos. Lagos: Federal Gov-
    ernment Printer, 1960.

_____. Report on the Registration of Title of Land in Lagos.
    Lagos: Federal Government Printer, 1957.

Storey, Bernard. Report of the Commission of Inquiry Into
    the Administration of the Lagos Town Council. Lagos:
    Government Printers, 1953.

Western Nigeria Government. Annual Report and Accounts
    for the Year Ended 31st March, 1959. Ibadan: Gov-
    ernment Printers, 1960.

_____. "Local Government Law" (Cap. 68). Ibadan:
    Government Printers, 1962.

Western Nigeria Government. Western Nigeria Development Plan, 1962-1968. Ibadan: Government Printers, 1962.

Books and Articles

Action Group. Lagos Belongs to the West. Ibadan: Action Group Secretariat, 1964.

Adebo, S. O., and Phillipson, Sydney. The Nigerianization of the Civil Service. Lagos: 1954.

Adeleye, T. O., and Oyediran, A. O. Report of Local Government Field Trip Assignment, Egbado, Badagry Division. Ibadan: Institute of Administration (University of Ife), 1965.

Awa, Eme O. Federal Government in Nigeria. Berkeley: University of California Press, 1964.

Awolowo, Obafemi. Path to Nigerian Freedom. London: Faber and Faber, 1947.

Azikiwe, Nnamdi. The Development of Political Parties in Nigeria. London: Commissioner for Eastern Nigeria, 1957.

Bascom, William R. Independent Nigeria: Portrait of an African State. Berkeley: University of California Press, 1960.

_____. "Urbanization Among the Yoruba," American Journal of Sociology, Vol. LX (1955).

Blitz, L. Franklin. The Politics and Administration of Nigerian Government. New York: Frederick A. Praeger, 1965.

Bretton, Henry L. Power and Stability in Nigeria. New York: Frederick A. Praeger, 1962.

Coleman, James S. Nigeria: Background to Nationalism. Berkeley: University of California Press, 1958.

Comhaire-Sylvain, S. "Associations on the Basis of Origin in Lagos," American Catholic Sociological Review, Vol. XI, No. 4 (December, 1950).

Ezera, Kalu. Constitutional Developments in Nigeria. Cambridge, Eng.: Cambridge University Press, 1964.

Harris, P. J. Local Government in Southern Nigeria. Cambridge, Eng.: Cambridge University Press, 1957.

Holland, S. W. C. "Recent Developments in Local Government in Eastern Nigeria," Journal of Local Administration Overseas, Vol. II, No. 1 (January, 1963).

International Bank for Reconstruction and Development. The Economic Development of Nigeria. Baltimore: Johns Hopkins University Press, 1955.

Lloyd, P. C. "The Development of Political Parties in Western Nigeria," American Political Science Review, XLIX (September, 1955), 693-708.

Marris, Peter. Family and Social Change in an African City. London: Routledge and Kegan Paul, 1961.

Ottenberg, Simon. British and Indigenous Practices in Local Government in Nigeria. Seattle: University of Washington, 1964. (Mimeo.)

Smythe, Hugh H. and Mabel M. The New Nigerian Elite. Palo Alto: Stanford University Press, 1960.

Tugbiyele, E. A. "Local Government in Nigeria," Journal of Local Administration Overseas, Vol. I, No. 4 (October, 1962).

UNESCO. Social Implications of Industrialization and Urbanization in Africa South of the Sahara. International African Institute, 1956.

United Nations. Workshop on Urbanization in Africa. SEM/URB/AF/1-20. Report and Working Papers. New York: Economic Commission for Africa, 1962.

Yesufu, T. M. Industrial Relations in Nigeria. London: Oxford University Press, 1962.

_____. "Manpower and Economic Development in Nigeria." Working Paper, Problems of Accelerated Growth and Manpower Planning in Developing Countries. Cairo: Institute of National Planning, 1962.

ABOUT THE AUTHORS

Babatunde A. Williams is Associate Professor in Government and Political Science at the School of Social Studies of the University of Lagos, Nigeria. His broad teaching experience includes that as Assistant Professor at Northern Illinois and Roosevelt Universities in the United States. He has lectured in government and economics at several other universities in Great Britain and West Africa.

Dr. Williams was formerly Senior Research Fellow at the Institute of Administration in Ibadan, Nigeria. A long-time resident of Lagos, he engaged in extensive research on government organization and administrative practices there during 1964.

Having studied at the University of Wisconsin, Dr. Williams received his Ph. D. degree from the University of Illinois.

Annmarie Hauck Walsh is a member of the research staff of the Institute of Public Administration, New York, and director of its International Urban Studies Project. She has participated in a wide range of studies at the Institute dealing with urban affairs, including urban transportation and outdoor recreation resources in American metropolitan areas.

During three years of research in comparative urban administration, she has traveled in Europe and Africa and participated in several field studies.

Mrs. Walsh was formerly editor of Metropolitan Area Problems: News and Digest. She has studied comparative politics and government at Smith College, the University of Geneva, and Columbia University.